RAMEN MADE SIMPLE

RAMEN
MADE SIMPLE

A Step-by-Step Guide

CHRIS TOY

PHOTOGRAPHY BY ELYSA WEITALA

ROCKRIDGE
PRESS

Interior and Cover Designer: Carlos Esparza
Art Producer: Janice Ackerman
Editor: Anna Pulley
Production Editor: Matthew Burnett
Production Manager: Riley Hoffman

Photography: © 2021 Elysa Weitala. Food styling by Victoria Woollard.
Author photograph: Courtesy of Kerry Michaels, Flying Point Photography

ISBN: Print 978-1-64739-865-1 | eBook 978-1-64739-543-8
R0

This book is dedicated in memory of my father,
Alfred M. Toy, who introduced me to late-night ramen
slurping so I could do the same with my children.
Thanks, Dad!

CONTENTS

INTRODUCTION

Making instant ramen with my father is a favorite childhood memory. On Saturday nights, after my mother and sister went to bed, Dad and I watched *The Twilight Zone*. Of course, I was too creeped out to go right to sleep. So we opened a few packages of instant ramen, with the foil flavor packets, and immersed them in bowls of hot water covered by dinner plates. In minutes, we were slurping tasty noodles before I happily headed off to bed.

Along with many other students, I continued my instant ramen habit throughout college for meals any time of day, including late-night snacks. The addition of homemade broth, eggs, vegetables, and slices of meat or fish provided affordable, tasty meals through graduate school and into my early years as a teacher.

As my own children grew, I enjoyed creating ramen memories with them. Whether it was a simple bowl of noodles and broth for a late-night treat or a hearty meal with eggs, vegetables, meat, and fresh garnishes, slurping bowls of steaming ramen brought us together. It is still a favorite when they visit and often on the menu for Sunday brunch.

While traveling as a consultant, I made it a point to ask my hosts which neighborhood restaurants the locals frequented to get the best homemade food. Noodle restaurants, or ramen-ya, were always among the favorite recommendations in Japan, the Philippines, Malaysia, and Thailand. I can say that, without exception, these often very small, basic eateries served up some of the best-tasting meals. Maybe it was the firm, freshly cut slippery noodles, or the savory bone broth that had been boiled for hours the previous day. Perhaps it was the tender sliced pork and fresh crispy vegetables that reminded me of home and family. Although the common denominator in all ramen is noodles and broth, it was always fun and exciting to see and taste the wide range of ramen recipes and ingredients from different regions.

Little did my father and I realize as we shared those simple packets of dried noodles back in the 1970s that ramen would soon become an iconic Japanese cultural staple and one of the most popular foods in the world. For me, slurping ramen is the tastiest comfort food, reminding me of home and time with my family—even when those memories are long ago and I am far away.

My hope in writing this book is that you, the reader and cook, will use these recipes to create many new memories with family and friends while sharing steaming bowls of rich broth, tasty toppings, and noisily slurping ramen noodles.

ONE

THE SIMPLE ART OF RAMEN

A Ramen Haiku
Umami flavors
warm steam rises from hot bowls
slippery noodles

Ramen is perhaps the most popular Japanese dish around the world. As is often the case with traditional recipes, ramen's story is intriguing; the basics are simple, and the variations are many. In this chapter, you will learn about ramen's Chinese origins and Japanese history from its inception to the explosion of ramen noodle restaurants in Japan and worldwide. I'll also share some simplified guidelines for making fresh homemade ramen, and call out some tools and ingredients you will need—or choose to obtain—depending on how involved you want to get in creating your own signature ramen.

THE HISTORY OF RAMEN

Although it's now an iconic staple of Japanese cuisine, ramen's roots originated in China. Travelers from China brought wheat noodles to Japan in the 1800s and these were called *shina* or *chuka soba*. The word "ramen" comes from the Chinese word for noodles, *la mian*.

In the 1900s, Chinese immigrants working in Yokohama's Chinatown in Japan prepared noodles with broth, providing laborers with quick, cheap meals flavored with sauces or "tare." Toppings of meat, fish, eggs, and vegetables were added, resembling the ramen bowls we enjoy today.

During World War II, Japan's rice crop declined, creating famine conditions. The United States exported wheat to Japan, thinking the Japanese would make bread. Since they were more familiar with noodles, the Japanese used the flour to make them, expanding ramen's popularity beyond Chinatown.

The spread of ramen in Japan, and its migration to college campuses around the world, accelerated in the 1960s with Momofuku Ando's invention of instant ramen. He discovered that flash-frying fresh noodles preserved them, enabling ramen to be prepared in minutes by soaking the noodles in hot water. Ando launched Nissin, the world's largest producer of instant ramen. He transformed ramen from a quick, inexpensive meal in Japan to one of the world's most popular foods.

THE FORMULA FOR BUILDING A BOWL

Here's a simplified version of the process of making ramen.

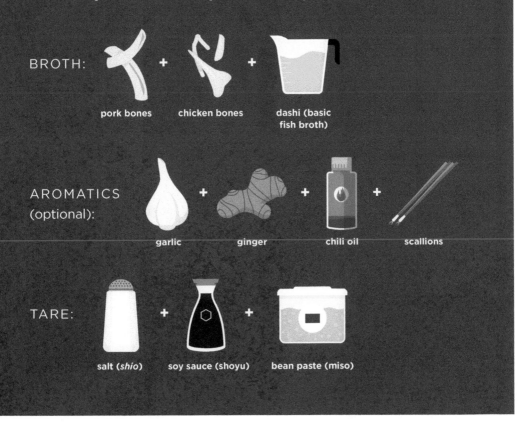

BROTH: pork bones + chicken bones + dashi (basic fish broth)

AROMATICS (optional):   garlic + ginger + chili oil + scallions

TARE: salt (*shio*) + soy sauce (shoyu) + bean paste (miso)

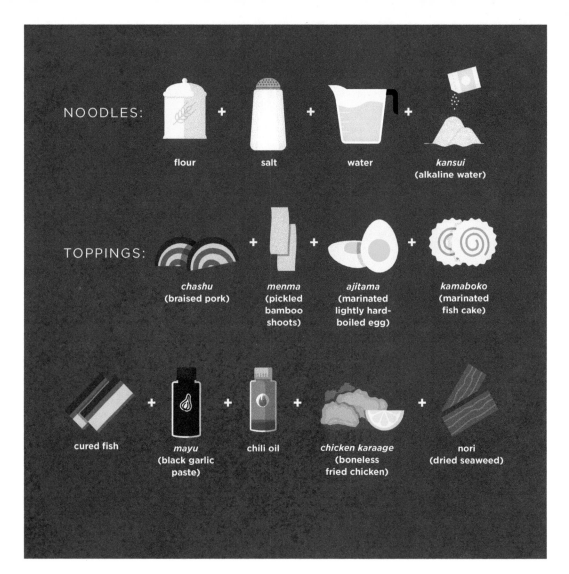

NOODLES: flour + salt + water + *kansui* (alkaline water)

TOPPINGS: *chashu* (braised pork) + *menma* (pickled bamboo shoots) + *ajitama* (marinated lightly hard-boiled egg) + *kamaboko* (marinated fish cake)

cured fish + *mayu* (black garlic paste) + chili oil + *chicken karaage* (boneless fried chicken) + nori (dried seaweed)

BROTH + TARE + NOODLES + TOPPINGS = RAMEN

At its simplest, ramen consists of noodles and broth. It can be as easy as peeling the foil on a cup of noodles, pouring in boiling water, and waiting three minutes. Or, you can prepare the broth overnight, roll out fresh noodles, slow-roast pork, prepare a tare seasoning, and assemble the ingredients for a bowl of fresh ramen. Depending on how involved you want to get, and with time, a few tools, and some effort, this book will guide you to making steaming bowls of homemade ramen so that you can create your own memories with family and friends.

A RAMEN CHEF'S TOOLS

Homemade ramen doesn't require many specialized tools. But here are some essentials, and a few specialty items, to help speed things up and get you started.

Chopsticks: Use longer chopsticks for cooking, stirring, and arranging your ingredients in the bowl. Smaller chopsticks are used in combination with soup spoons to eat.

Fine-mesh strainer: Use this to skim and strain broth. It can also be used to drain your cooked noodles before placing them in bowls of steaming broth. This should be wide enough to sit comfortably across your stockpot.

Food processor: Using a 5- to 8-cup food processor can help you quickly prepare enough noodle dough for four bowls.

Immersion blender: Used to emulsify strained broth prepared in a pressure cooker, for rich, cloudy Tonkotsu-style broth.

Ladles: Use a large soup ladle for broth and a smaller one for distributing tare.

Large stockpot: Use a 6- to 8-quart stockpot for 6 to 8 cups of broth. You'll need room in the pot for bones and aromatics plus enough space for them to move about as the broth boils.

Noodle strainer: Optional, but this basket enables you to boil and serve individual helpings of noodles without dumping the boiling water.

Pressure cooker: This significantly reduces the time and energy it takes to make ramen bone broth. With a 6-quart pressure cooker, you can prepare enough broth for four large bowls of ramen in less than 2 hours, whereas on the stovetop it can take 12 hours.

Ramen bowls: Using wide bowls with steep sides will allow the noodles and ingredients to float on top of the broth. Steep sides will make it easier to drink the broth from the bowl.

Saucepan: Use a 4- to 6-quart saucepan to boil enough noodles for four bowls.

Skillet: Use a 9- to 12-inch skillet for lightly browning or searing meat, fish, or vegetables.

Soup spoons: Use large soup spoons in combination with chopsticks to lift noodles, toppings, and broth closer for slurping. You can use silverware soup spoons or the Asian-style stone/ceramic ramen spoons called *chirirenge* or just *renge*.

CREATING YOUR PANTRY: A RAMENCYCLOPEDIA

Here is a short list of common ingredients used in making ramen. Keep in mind that there are hundreds of possible ingredients depending on tastes, region, and creativity. Many of these can be found in grocery stores, Asian markets, or online.

Dashi: Broth made from fish flakes, konbu (kelp), and shiitake mushrooms. Make it from scratch or purchase a store-bought version.

Garlic: Fresh is best, but a jar of refrigerated garlic works.

Ginger: Fresh is best but a jar of refrigerated ginger also works.

Kansui (alkaline water): Used in making ramen noodles, this ingredient gives the noodles their firm, chewy texture and yellow color.

Katsuobushi: Fermented, dried bonito tuna flakes used along with konbu to make dashi broth.

Konbu (also spelled "kombu"): Dried sea kelp. A key ingredient in dashi.

Mirin: A sweet rice cooking wine.

Nori: Dried sheets of seaweed cut into strips for topping ramen.

Sake: A dry rice wine that can be used in marinades and for flavoring broth.

Scallion: A key aromatic used for flavoring broth and tare. It can also be used as a garnish.

Shiitake mushrooms: Mushrooms provide the umami flavor for broths and tare. They can be used fresh or dried.

Soy sauce: Made by fermenting soybeans, wheat, salt, and water. Soy sauce, or Japanese *shoyu*, imparts a salty, sweet, umami flavor. It's used in tare and for marinades.

Wakame: A dried sea vegetable—available whole and powered—sprinkled into the broth just before being served, adding a briny flavor.

10 SIMPLE RULES FOR MAKING RAMEN

When it comes to making ramen, there are no official "rules." That said, the following guidelines ensure creating your delicious bowls is a simple, stress-free experience, and are based on my experience as a chef, international food consultant, and avid ramen enthusiast.

1. **Decide how much time you want to spend.** In 10 minutes, you can make reasonably good ramen with instant noodles, bouillon packets, eggs, and vegetables. Or, you can spend two days making fresh-cut noodles, boiling bone broth, marinating boiled eggs, and braising melt-in-your-mouth chashu.

2. **Gather all components before assembling your bowls of ramen.** Noodles, broth, tare, toppings, bowls, spoons, and chopsticks should be present and accounted for on your countertop. Timing matters!

3. **Don't overcook the noodles.** You want your cooked noodles to be slightly chewy. Avoid letting them sit in the broth for more than a couple of minutes before slurping them.

4. **It's okay to use store-bought noodles.** The most common option is buying dried noodles from grocery stores, Asian markets, or online. There is a wide variety of noodles available including gluten-free and low-carb options. You can also find fresh or frozen noodles in Asian markets.

5. **There are many options for broths.** The simplest option is using the packets accompanying instant ramen. But a healthier, additive-free, and almost-as-fast way is to prepare your own quick broth. One of my favorites is the Better Than Bouillon brand, found in most grocery stores, because it has no artificial additives or MSG and is available in different varieties for omnivores and vegetarians.

6. **A pressure cooker can make great broth from scratch in less than 2 hours.** The next fastest way to prepare your own broth from scratch is by boiling chicken, pork, or beef bones in a pressure cooker (see chapter 3 for broth recipes).

7. **Counterbalance your noodles and broth.** The heavier the broth, the thinner the noodles should be; for thinner broths, use thicker noodles.

8. **Beyond the aromatics, never add seasoning to the broth.** Seasoning comes from adding the tare and seasoned oil to each bowl of ramen as it is assembled.

9. **Tare seasoning can be as simple as bottled sauce.** There are ramen lovers who make tare with miso, soy sauce, garlic, and hot pepper oil. And there are others who season their noodles with soy sauce and ketchup. It's up to you how simple you want to go. I'll share several tare recipes with you (see chapter 3). As always, feel free to create your own special sauces.

10. **The final rule is: You make the rules.** Other than making sure you do not overcook the noodles, anything goes! Try a wide variety of noodles. Make your own with different thicknesses, herbs, and flavors. Experiment with different broths. Create unique tare seasonings to add to your bowls of noodles. Experiment with different toppings. And most important, have fun!

TWO

FOOLPROOF RAMEN: A STEP-BY-STEP GUIDE

Ramen's building blocks are broth, tare, noodles, and toppings. In this chapter, you'll learn about these essential elements and how to easily create a perfectly balanced, delicious bowl of ramen at home. We'll discuss types of broth, which gives ramen its subtle background taste; different tares, the primary seasoning agent in ramen; how to make the signature chewy noodles; and learn about some of the most common meat, seafood, and vegetable toppings, which add color, taste, texture, and nutrition.

BROTH

Broth is the foundation of ramen. Boiling meat, vegetables, and aromatics like ginger, garlic, and scallions creates a lightly flavored base for your homemade ramen. Broth that is heavy and cloudy is *kotteri*, while light and clear broth is *assari*. Kotteri broth is made by vigorously boiling bones and other ingredients for several hours. Assari broth is made by simmering ingredients, usually for a shorter time.

There are five flavors of ramen broth. They may be kotteri or assari depending on the ingredients: Shio, or salt broth, is the oldest and is often assari. Light brown shoyu broth is soy sauce–based. Miso broth with fermented soybeans tends to be kotteri. Tonkotsu is made by boiling bones, and is kotteri, as it's the cloudiest and heaviest. The most recent type of kotteri broth is *kare*, or curried broth. Mix and match ingredients to suit your dietary needs and tastes!

Broth Prep and Troubleshooting Tips

- Plan a day or two ahead if you're making broth from scratch, especially if it's a bone broth.
- Time broth-making to coincide with roasting meat or vegetables for dinner. Use the scraps for broth.
- For extra flavor, brown the aromatics, meat, and vegetables before using them to make broth.

BROTH MADE SIMPLE

CLEAR CHICKEN BROTH

Stockpot + water + bones, aromatics, and konbu

bring to a simmer (2 to 3 hours)

strain ← **skim** ← **discard solids**

CLOUDY CHICKEN BROTH

Stockpot + water + bones, aromatics, and konbu

bring to a boil (3 hours)

strain ← **skim** ← **discard solids**

TONKOTSU PORK BROTH

Stockpot + water + pork bones, pig's feet, and aromatics

boil on stovetop (6 to 8 hours) or use a pressure cooker

discard solids

water + boil + skim

strain

FISH BROTH

Stockpot + water

bring to a boil

turn off + bonito flakes and konbu + steep (up to 20 minutes)

discard solids

strain

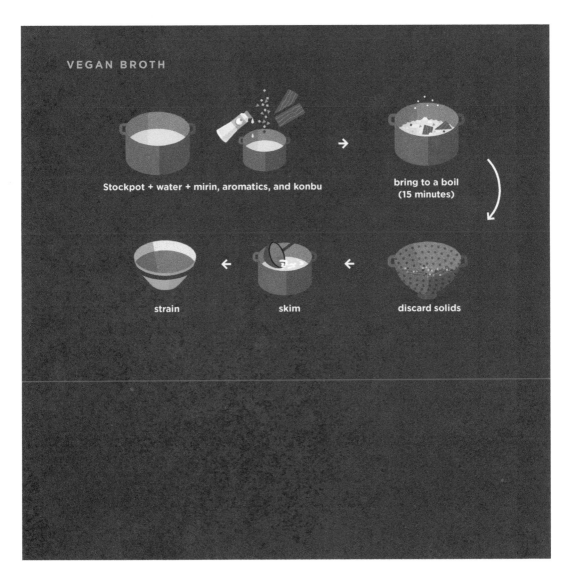

VEGAN BROTH

Stockpot + water + mirin, aromatics, and konbu

bring to a boil
(15 minutes)

discard solids

skim

strain

- When making bone or pork broth, cover the bones with water and parboil for 10 minutes. This removes blood and scum from the meat and bones that can give a grayish-brown color to the broth. Dump the water, then start your broth.
- Short on time? Use canned broth. This won't work for tonkotsu broth, as this broth gets its unique characteristics from boiling bones, but it will for other styles.
- Using bouillon? Make it half-strength. It's very salty and contains other flavorings.
- Freeze leftover broth in double zip-top bags. It will last for several months.

TARE

The dominant flavor in ramen comes from tare (pronounced tah-*ray*), a concentrated sauce placed in the bowl before other ingredients are added. There are four types of tare named for their dominant flavors. Shio is based on salt. It may have lemon, seaweed, and dashi flavoring. Shoyu is based on soy sauce. It may have similar flavors, including fish paste, mushrooms, mirin, sugar, and vinegar. Miso tare is fermented bean paste, plus soy sauce, mirin, garlic, ginger, and ground red pepper. Kare, or curry tare, uses Japanese powdered curry as its flavor base, along with dashi, soy sauce, and mirin.

As with the ramen broth bases, you can mix and match the ingredients to create your own types of tare. Noodle houses, or ramen-ya, often develop their own signature tare, keeping the recipes secret. So go ahead and develop your own secret sauce. Just remember to take notes!

TARE MADE SIMPLE

SHIO TARE

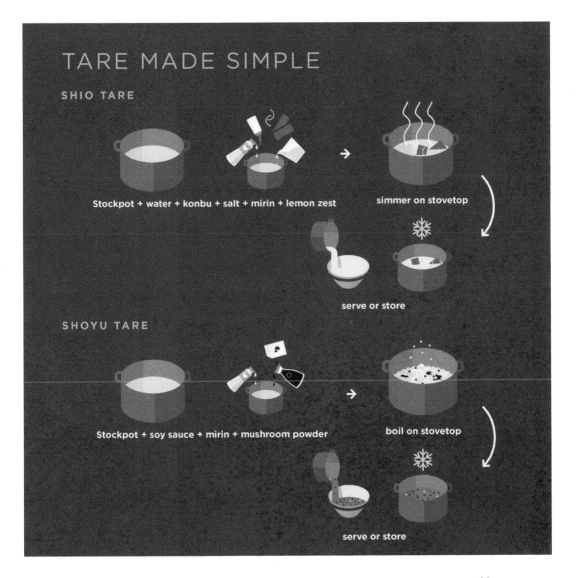

Stockpot + water + konbu + salt + mirin + lemon zest → simmer on stovetop

serve or store

SHOYU TARE

Stockpot + soy sauce + mirin + mushroom powder → boil on stovetop

serve or store

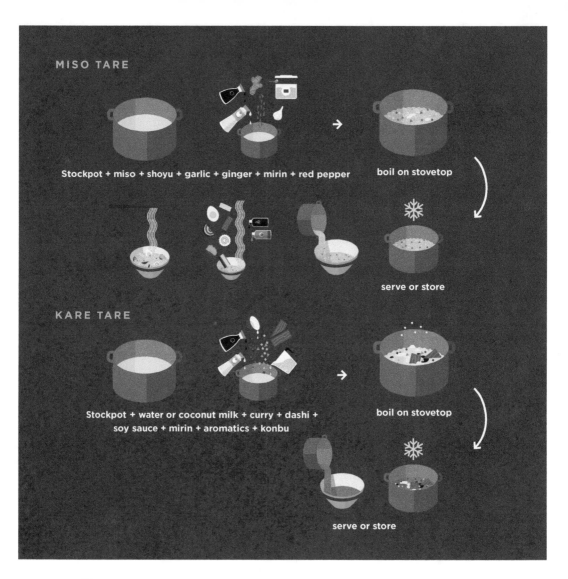

MISO TARE

Stockpot + miso + shoyu + garlic + ginger + mirin + red pepper

boil on stovetop

serve or store

KARE TARE

Stockpot + water or coconut milk + curry + dashi +
soy sauce + mirin + aromatics + konbu

boil on stovetop

serve or store

Tare Prep and Troubleshooting Tips

- For the best results, prepare tare the day before you want to serve it so that flavors can develop.
- Tare will cook faster with less splatter if you use a deep, wide pan. Deep sides contain the splatter and greater width increases evaporation.
- If you don't have mirin, you can substitute 2 parts sake plus 1 part sugar, or white grape juice.
- If you don't have sake, you can use Shaoxing wine or dry sherry.
- You can substitute tamari for soy sauce. Tamari is less salty and has a deeper umami flavor.
- With lemon zest, avoid using the white pith just under the yellow peel, as it is bitter. Lime zest is also a tasty substitute, or try orange zest.
- For a clear assari ramen, you can use a coffee filter to remove the solids in the shio and shoyu tare. This is not possible with the miso and kare tare as the solids provide body and much of the flavor.
- Tare will keep in an airtight container in the refrigerator for about two weeks.

NOODLES

The key to ramen noodles is that they must be firm and chewy, never soft and soggy. Ramen noodles are primarily wheat noodles, eggless, and made with water, flour, salt, and kansui, an alkaline water containing potassium carbonate and sodium bicarbonate. Kansui reacts with the gluten in the flour, making a dense, elastic dough. This gives ramen noodles their yellow color and firm chewiness.

A wide variety of dried ramen noodles is readily available in grocery stores, Asian markets, and online. Let's take a brief tour of store-bought noodles before we look at simple homemade noodles.

Store-Bought Noodles

Ramen noodles may be thin, thick, straight, or wavy. If you can find fresh or frozen noodles in the store, and are planning to use them within the week, buy them. They are next best to making your own. Some well-known brands are Sun Noodle, Hakubaku, and Meister. You can also find many gluten-free versions now, including yam-based, low-carb shirataki noodles made by Miracle Noodle. Some Asian markets will have locally made noodles as well.

The choice of dried noodles can be overwhelming. The simplest option is to buy plain noodles without the flavor packets. Ocean's Halo, Hime, Hakubaku, and Ka-Me are all reliable brands and have a variety of thin, thick, curly, and gluten-free options.

Homemade Noodles

Making fresh noodles is amazingly simple. It involves four ingredients, and depending on the tools you have on hand, it can be as fast as 10 minutes. In chapter 3, I've included a recipe for Homemade Ramen Noodles (page 46). You'll want a high-protein flour, such as bread flour, which makes for a denser dough

NOODLES MADE SIMPLE

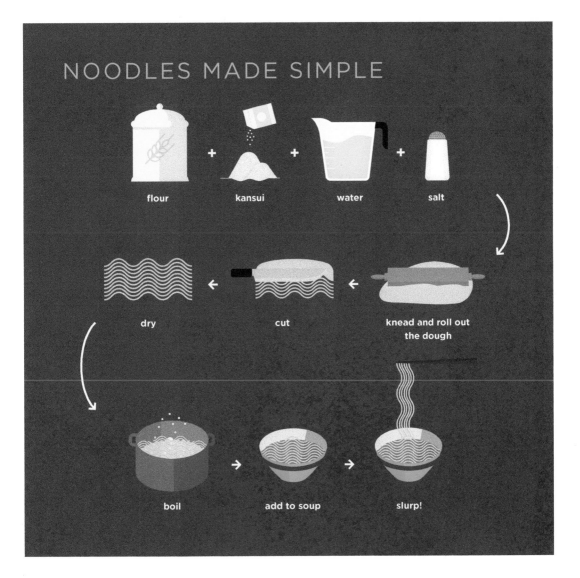

flour + kansui + water + salt

knead and roll out the dough → cut → dry → boil → add to soup → slurp!

and chewier noodles. The only ingredient that may be unfamiliar is kansui, which is available in some grocery stores, Asian markets, and online. Adding salt to the dough strengthens the gluten, making the dough more elastic and the noodles chewier. Salt also adds flavor.

Noodle Prep Tips and Troubleshooting

- Ideally you'll want to make the noodles a day in advance to give the gluten in the dough time to develop and to let the noodles dry a bit.
- The key is to get the consistency of the dough right. Ramen dough is very dense and takes some time and effort to knead and roll by hand. Using hot water speeds up the process of forming gluten and keeps the dough softer.
- The fastest way to get the consistency right is to use a food processor. When processing the dough it should look like uncooked couscous, small pellets of dough. If it forms a ball or the pellets stick together, the dough is too wet. If you pinch a teaspoon of pellets between your fingers and they crumble, the dough is too dry. When you've gotten close to the ideal texture, add water or flour a teaspoon at a time until it's right.
- Let the dough rest right in the food processor or in an airtight container for 20 minutes to let the gluten form before rolling it out.
- Make sure the water is already boiling before placing the noodles in the water. Test them constantly by biting into a strand, as it is a matter of seconds between them being just right or soggy.

- If you are serving a crowd, it's not a bad idea to slightly undercook the noodles before removing them from the boiling water and placing them into bowls of steaming broth, where they'll finish cooking.

TOPPINGS AND FLAVORINGS

There is something for everyone with ramen, especially when it comes to toppings. There's no limit to the number and combination of toppings possible, but here's a ramen chef's dozen to get you started.

Ajitama: A lightly hard-boiled egg that has been marinated in soy sauce and mirin overnight. It is cut in half, revealing a soft custard-like yolk.

Aonegi: Chopped green scallions. If you cut them at an angle and give them a squeeze before adding them to the ramen, they will spread their flavor into the bowl.

Bean sprouts: A fast way to add some cool, crunchy, healthy sweetness.

Chashu: Braised or slow-roasted pork marinated in soy sauce and brown sugar.

Corn: Try young, sweet white corn. Fresh off the cob is best, but frozen works well, too. Put a pat of butter or fat on the corn, or brown the corn a bit before placing it in the bowl.

Kamaboko: Also known as naruto. This is a sliced, processed fish cake that has been steamed and refrigerated. Sirimi or artificial crab and lobster are the closest thing to it in grocery stores.

Menma: Bamboo shoots that have been dried and fermented. They are soaked in dashi before being added to ramen. They are sometimes referred to as Chinese bamboo.

Mushrooms: Sliced shiitake mushrooms add umami flavor. They can be fresh or dried and soaked. Reconstituted mushrooms have a strong flavor and chewier texture than fresh ones. Other types of mushrooms include enoki, oyster, and tree or wood ear.

Negi: Leeks. Thinly slice and squeeze them before either frying them in some sesame oil or butter.

Niku soboro: Ground meat of any kind, including seafood, that has been stir-fried in soy sauce, spices, and mirin.

Nori: This seaweed paper topping is usually cut into strips and sprinkled on top of the other ingredients, adding a little texture and a briny flavor.

Sesame oil: This tasty, nutty oil can be light yellow, toasted brown, or spicy red. It may be drizzled in the bottom of the bowl with the tare or as a garnish.

Shiraganegi: Thinly sliced strips of the white parts of scallions, which have a stronger flavor than green scallions.

TOPPINGS AND FLAVORINGS MADE SIMPLE

Although ramen topping options may be endless, here are a few combinations to get you started.

TONKOTSU RAMEN	VEGETARIAN SHOYU RAMEN	VEGAN SHIO RAMEN	KARE RAMEN	MISO RAMEN
pork belly	tofu	seitan	niku soboro	aonegi
scallions	enoki	nori	menma	kamaboko
ginger	bok choy	mayu	corn	tree ears
nori	ajitama	chili oil	bean sprouts	ajitama

Topping Prep Tips and Troubleshooting

- As you're planning the contents of your ramen bowl toppings, consider the balance of textures and flavors. You don't want too many strong flavors that will clash and drown out subtle ingredients. Simple can go a long way. One or two proteins, two vegetables, one garnish, and perhaps a dash of flavoring provide plenty of variety.
- Prepare toppings in advance and lay them out so that you can focus on quickly assembling the bowls. If you have chashu or other cooked meats, you'll want to sear or heat them up, too.

- All vegetables, garnishes, and flavorings should be cut up and organized for assembly.
- When making ajitama, marinate the eggs for 4 hours (or overnight), but not longer than 3 days, as they can get too salty.

BRINGING IT ALL TOGETHER

You're almost ready to start slurping. Here's your step-by-step guide to assembling ramen.

1. Choose the right bowls. Shallow, oven-safe bowls with steep sides are best, especially if you want to pick up the bowl and drink the broth after a couple of helpings of noodles. Heat the oven-safe bowls before assembling them by placing them in your oven on low (200°F) for 15 minutes or in your microwave for 1 or 2 minutes.

2. While the bowls heat, bring your broth to a simmer, and in another pot, boil water to cook the noodles. Place the noodles in the boiling water so that they just finish cooking when you are ready to place them in bowls of hot broth.

3. While the noodles are cooking, place a small ladle of tare in the center of each heated bowl. If you are using flavored oil, add a few drops now.

4. Pour about 1 cup of broth into each bowl, leaving room for noodles and toppings. If your tare is a paste, whisk it into the broth.

5. Place your perfectly cooked noodles into the steaming broth, spreading them out a little.

6. Place heavier toppings, such as meat and eggs, into the bowl next.

7. Add raw or cooked vegetables, followed by any garnishes. If you are using nori, add that last, as it can get soggy quickly.

8. Provide a soup spoon along with chopsticks (if using) for each person.

9. Be sure to slurp!

ABOUT THE RECIPES

Each recipe from chapters 4 to 8 incorporates several of the Master Recipes (chapter 3), enabling you to create dozens of unique ramen soup bowls. Each recipe also includes a variation at the end, to double your ramen options and help spark your own signature bowls. Once you become familiar with the key components and how to make them, you'll be ready to invent endless variations of your own signature ramen bowls. I also include cooking tips, prep tips, storage tips, and ways to make the recipe even simpler. Finally, I note any special characteristics of each recipe such as whether it's vegetarian or vegan, or conveniently one-pot.

AJITAMA EGGS, PAGE 52

THREE

MASTER RECIPES

The following master recipes incorporate the four building blocks of ramen (broth, tare, noodles, and toppings). Mixing and matching these combinations allows for an infinite variety of ramen bowls and will help you create all the recipes in this book. More important, you'll be ready to change up and add to the recipes, creating your own signature inventions.

CLEAR CHICKEN BROTH

Makes 4 bowls (about 4 cups)   **Prep time: 15 minutes / Cook time: 3 hours**

Clear chicken broth tests a ramen chef's technical and aesthetic skills. Attaining the complex flavor combination of vegetables, chicken, aromatics, and umami flavors while maintaining the clarity of the broth requires patience and practice. Shio or shoyu tare is often paired with this clear, assari-style broth, which keeps for three days in the fridge or three months in the freezer.

6 cups water

2 pounds bone-in
   chicken wings

4 to 6 scallions, green
   and white parts,
   coarsely chopped

1 medium yellow
   onion, diced

1 medium carrot, diced

6 garlic cloves, crushed

1 tablespoon (1-inch piece)
   fresh ginger, unpeeled and
   crushed

¼ ounce (4-inch
   square) konbu

1. In a large stockpot over high heat, bring the water to a boil, add the chicken wings and boil for 2 minutes.

2. With a fine-mesh strainer, skim off any foam and lower the heat to a simmer.

3. Add the scallions, onion, carrot, garlic, ginger, and konbu and simmer, uncovered, for 3 hours. Keep the temperature below 200°F.

4. Using a fine-mesh strainer, filter the broth and discard the solids. Serve the broth immediately, or store in an airtight container in the fridge and reheat as needed.

Mix it up: Adding a pound of ground chicken to the pot will make a richer broth. Instead of wings, you can substitute chicken feet (ask at the butcher counter, or an Asian market).

Cooking tip: A pressure cooker brings the cooking time down to 30 minutes. Reduce the amount of water by 2 cups. The broth will not boil in a pressure cooker, keeping the broth clear.

CLOUDY CHICKEN BROTH

Makes 4 bowls (about 4 cups)   Prep time: 15 minutes / Cook time: 3 hours

Tori paitan means "white chicken broth" in Japanese. It is the lesser-known cousin of tonkotsu, a creamy broth made with pork bones. Unlike the simmering process for making a clear, assari-style broth, here we use rapid boiling, which creates a cloudy, kotteri-type broth. A 3-pound chicken carcass can be substituted for the wings.

6 cups water	1 medium yellow	1 tablespoon (1-inch piece)
2 pounds bone-in	onion, diced	fresh ginger, unpeeled and
chicken wings	1 medium carrot, diced	crushed
1 pound ground chicken	6 garlic cloves, crushed	¼ ounce (4-inch
4 to 6 scallions, green and		square) konbu
white parts, minced		

1. In a large stockpot over high heat, bring the water to a boil, add the chicken wings, and boil for 2 minutes.
2. With a fine-mesh strainer, skim off any foam. Add the ground chicken, scallions, onion, carrot, garlic, ginger, and konbu to the pot and boil, uncovered, for 3 hours.
3. Using a fine-mesh strainer, filter the broth and discard the solids. Serve the broth immediately, or store in an airtight container in the fridge and reheat as needed.

Cooking tip: A pressure cooker reduces the cooking time to 1 hour. Reduce the water to 4 cups. After pressure cooking, remove the lid and boil the broth for 30 minutes to emulsify it. Or, you can use an immersion or regular blender to emulsify it.

FISH BROTH (DASHI)

Makes 4 bowls (about 5 cups)   **Prep time: 5 minutes / Cook time: 10 minutes**

Japanese fish broth (katsuo dashi) is one of the easiest broths to make, as it's similar to steeping a pot of tea. It is a clear, assari-style broth and, at its simplest, has only two ingredients: bonito flakes and water. You can increase the umami flavor by adding other ingredients high in natural glutamates, such as dried mushrooms, konbu, dried shrimp, and dried sardines.

5 cups water

½ cup bonito flakes

¼ ounce (4-inch square) konbu

1. In a large stockpot over high heat, bring the water to a boil, then remove from the heat.

2. Add the bonito flakes and konbu and steep for 10 minutes.

3. With a fine-mesh strainer, filter the broth and discard the solids. Serve the broth immediately, or store in an airtight container in the fridge and reheat as needed.

Mix it up: Experiment by adding other kinds of dried seafood such as shrimp, sardines, scallops, and cuttlefish.

Cooking tip: This broth is best used within a day or two of being made.

TONKOTSU PORK BROTH

Makes 4 bowls (about 4 cups)   Prep time: 30 minutes / Cook time: 6 to 8 hours

Tonkotsu means "pork bone broth" in Japanese. This rich ramen broth is made by vigorously boiling pork bones for several hours. The boiling action draws out the collagen protein along with the flavor of the bones and meat.

1 pound pig's feet, cut into 2-inch pieces

1 pound pig neck bones, cut into chunks

10 cups water

2 tablespoons vegetable oil

1 medium yellow onion, diced

6 to 8 scallions, green and white parts, sliced

6 garlic cloves, crushed

1 tablespoon (1-inch piece) fresh ginger, unpeeled and crushed

1 (8-ounce) piece fat salt pork, quartered

1. In a large stockpot over high heat, cover the pig's feet and neck bones with the water and boil for 20 minutes. Drain the water.

2. Rinse the bones in cold water and wash out the pot. Return the bones to the pot.

3. Cover the bones with water 1 inch over their tops, bring to a boil, and using a fine-mesh strainer, skim off the foam.

4. In a large skillet, heat the oil over medium heat, add the onion, scallions, garlic, and ginger and brown, stirring frequently. Add the mixture to the boiling bones.

5. Add the salt pork to the pot. Cover and continue boiling for 6 to 8 hours. Maintain a rolling boil without the water boiling over, adding water periodically to keep the bones submerged.

6. When the broth is milky, filter it through a fine-mesh strainer. Discard the solids. Serve the broth immediately, or store in an airtight container in the fridge and reheat as needed.

Mix it up: Add beef and chicken bones to the pork. You can also add 2 ounces of dried mushrooms to the boiling broth for extra umami.

Cooking tip: A pressure cooker brings the cooking time down to 3 hours. Reduce the water to 6 cups. After pressure cooking, boil the broth, uncovered, for 30 minutes to emulsify it. Or, you can use an immersion or regular blender to emulsify it.

VEGAN BROTH

Makes 4 bowls (about 4 cups)   Prep time: 5 minutes / Cook time: 15 minutes

This broth uses the classic flavor base of ginger, garlic, and scallions. The savory fifth flavor, umami, comes from mushrooms and konbu, creating a tasty clear, assari-style broth. Your omnivore guests won't miss the meat at all!

4 cups water

¼ cup mirin

3 garlic cloves, crushed

1 tablespoon (1-inch piece) fresh ginger, unpeeled and crushed

4 scallions, green and white parts, cut into 1-inch pieces

1 ounce dried shiitake mushrooms, sliced

¼ ounce (4-inch square) konbu

1. In a large stockpot over high heat, bring the water and mirin to a simmer.
2. Add the garlic, ginger, scallions, mushrooms, and konbu and continue to simmer for 15 minutes.
3. With a fine-mesh strainer, filter the broth and discard the solids. Serve the broth immediately, or store in an airtight container in the fridge and reheat as needed.

Mix it up: Browning or lightly charring the garlic, ginger, and scallions in vegetable oil or sesame oil adds depth of flavor. You can also spice it up by adding dried red chili flakes or spicy sesame oil.

Cooking tip: You can substitute ¼ cup of sake and 2 tablespoons of sugar for the mirin. No mirin or sake? A sweet white, dessert, or ice wine can work.

MISO TARE

Makes enough to flavor 4 bowls (about ½ cup)   **Prep time: 5 minutes / Cook time: 5 minutes**

Miso is made by fermenting soybeans, salt, and sugar for many months, until it develops into a strong, salty, umami-rich paste. Ginger, garlic, tamari, and spicy or toasted sesame oil are added in order to balance out the strength of the miso.

½ cup white miso

1 tablespoon (1-inch piece) fresh ginger, unpeeled, crushed, and chopped

3 garlic cloves, crushed and chopped

2 tablespoons tamari or soy sauce

¼ cup mirin

1 teaspoon spicy sesame oil

1. In a small saucepan over low heat, combine the miso, ginger, garlic, tamari, mirin, and sesame oil.

2. Cook, stirring, for 5 minutes until everything is evenly mixed. Serve.

Prep tip: Try different kinds of miso. Red has the strongest flavor, followed by yellow, and white. You can use a blended miso as well.

SHIO TARE

Makes enough to flavor 4 bowls (about 1 cup)

Prep time: 5 minutes / Cook time: 5 minutes, plus overnight to marinate

Shio means "salt" in Japanese. This simple salt-and-konbu combo brings out the flavor in chicken and pork broths. The lemon zest gives the tare a bright, tangy taste that will wake up your taste buds.

1 cup water	Zest of 2 lemons	¼ cup kosher salt
½ ounce (two 4-inch squares) konbu	Juice of 2 lemons (about 4 tablespoons)	

1. In a small saucepan over high heat, bring the water and konbu to a simmer.
2. Stir in the lemon zest, lemon juice, and salt until the salt dissolves.
3. Let the mixture cool to room temperature before placing in an airtight container and refrigerating overnight.
4. With a fine-mesh strainer, filter the broth and discard the solids. Serve.

Mix it up: Experiment with lime, orange, and grapefruit zest.

SHOYU TARE

Makes enough to flavor 4 bowls (about 1½ cups)

Prep time: 10 minutes / Cook time: 10 minutes

One of the world's oldest sauces, shoyu (soy sauce) is made by fermenting soybeans in a mixture of salt, sugar, and water with a special mold fungus, aspergillus, for up to a year. The fermentation process produces a dark, salty-sweet condiment filled with what is known as the fifth taste, umami. Shoyu tare adds complexity and additional umami with the addition of such ingredients as mushrooms, konbu, ginger, and garlic. Use tamari if you'd like a slightly less salty tare.

1 cup soy sauce or tamari

½ cup mirin

¼ cup dark brown sugar, packed

6 garlic cloves, crushed and chopped

1 tablespoon (1-inch piece) fresh ginger, unpeeled, crushed, and chopped

6 scallions, green and white parts, roughly chopped

1 teaspoon spicy sesame oil

1. In a medium saucepan over medium-high heat, combine the soy sauce, mirin, brown sugar, garlic, ginger, scallions, and sesame oil and bring to a boil.
2. Reduce the heat to medium and continue boiling and stirring for 10 minutes.
3. Using a fine-mesh strainer, filter the broth and discard the solids. Serve.

Mix it up: For more umami flavor, add 1 ounce of sliced dried mushrooms or 1 tablespoon of mushroom powder. You can also add 1 teaspoon of fish sauce to increase the umami, but it won't be vegan. For less heat, substitute toasted sesame oil for the spicy sesame oil.

KARE (CURRY) COCONUT TARE

Makes enough to flavor 4 bowls (about 2 cups)

Prep time: 10 minutes / Cook time: 10 minutes

Kare, or curry ramen, a recent development, was first made in 1965 in the city of Muroran on the island of Hokkaido, Japan. This tare is unique as the broth base can be coconut water or coconut milk, depending on whether you prefer a clear, assari-style broth or a heavier kotteri-style one. This version makes the latter.

- 1 (14-ounce) can coconut milk
- ¼ cup mirin
- ¼ ounce (4-inch square) konbu
- 2 scallions, green and white parts, roughly chopped
- 3 garlic cloves, crushed and chopped
- 1 tablespoon (1-inch piece) fresh ginger, unpeeled, crushed, and chopped
- 2 tablespoons Japanese curry powder
- 1 teaspoon spicy sesame oil
- 1 tablespoon white miso
- 2 tablespoons dark brown sugar, packed

1. In a medium saucepan over high heat, bring the coconut milk, mirin, konbu, and scallions to a low simmer.

2. Whisk in the garlic, ginger, curry powder, sesame oil, miso, and brown sugar and simmer for 10 minutes.

3. Using a fine-mesh strainer, filter the broth and discard the solids. Serve.

Mix it up: For a clear broth, use 14 ounces of coconut water in place of the coconut milk. One ounce of dried sliced mushrooms or 1 tablespoon of mushroom powder can also be added to increase flavor, as well as juice from 1 lemon or lime.

HOMEMADE RAMEN NOODLES

Makes enough for 4 bowls   **Prep time: 1 hour / Cook time: 2 minutes**

The Japanese word for noodle, "men," comes from the Chinese "mein," as in "lo mein" and "chow mein." This recipe takes a bit of time and effort depending on what tools you have (I recommend a food processor and pasta machine), but is well worth trying.

1 cup bread flour   1 tablespoon kosher salt
¼ cup warm water   1 tablespoon kansui

1. In a food processor, combine the flour, water, salt, and kansui and pulse until the mixture forms small pellets of dough similar to uncooked couscous. The pellets should not stick together until a pinch of the dough is pressed between your thumb and forefinger. This will take about 5 minutes. If you don't have a food processor, mix the ingredients in a medium bowl and knead until it is smooth and does not stick to your hands, about 20 minutes.

2. Place the dough in a plastic bag or wrap it in plastic. Let it rest for 30 minutes at room temperature.

3. Divide the dough into two balls. Flatten one with the palm of your hand. Use a pasta machine to roll and cut the dough to your desired thickness and width. Start with the thickest setting and run the dough through twice at each setting, folding the dough in half each time. Rolling and folding the dough with the machine kneads the dough much faster because the rollers exert much more force than your hands when working the dough. The dough will break up at first but will smooth out as you continue reducing

the thickness and folding. If you don't have a pasta machine, you can knead and roll by hand, but it's harder, as the dough is very dense. You can make the dough a little softer by increasing the water a bit. Flouring the board as you roll the softer dough will help firm it up as the dough gets thinner.

4. To cook, heat a large stockpot full of water over high heat and boil the noodles for 1 to 2 minutes. Drain and serve immediately.

Prep tip: The longer you let the dough rest the easier it will be to roll out due to the gluten formation. Warm, rested dough is easier to work than cold dough. If your dough is too dry and doesn't pinch together, add 1 teaspoon of water and process until the moisture is incorporated into the dough. If the dough forms a ball in the processor or sticks to your hands, add 1 teaspoon of flour and process until the flour is incorporated into the dough. Add water or flour in teaspoon or smaller increments as needed.

Mix it up: You can flavor the noodles by processing spices and aromatics in with the dry ingredients before adding water. Pepper, ginger, and garlic are good options.

CHASHU PORK

Makes 8 to 12 pieces

Prep time: 15 minutes / Cook time: 2 hours, plus overnight to marinate

Chashu is one of the most popular ramen toppings. And it's no wonder. The melt-in-your-mouth pork belly is tender, sweet, and full of umami. It takes a bit of time and planning to season and braise, but it's well worth the effort.

2 tablespoons vegetable oil

12 ounces pork belly, skin removed

2 scallions, green and white parts, cut into 1-inch pieces

1 tablespoon (1-inch piece) fresh ginger, unpeeled, crushed, and chopped

3 garlic cloves, crushed and chopped

⅓ cup mirin

⅓ cup soy sauce

⅔ cup water

¼ cup dark brown sugar, packed

1. In a heavy skillet, heat the oil on high heat. Starting with the fat side, sear both sides of the pork belly, about 5 minutes per side. Set aside.
2. In a large stockpot over high heat, combine the scallions, ginger, garlic, mirin, soy sauce, water, and brown sugar and bring to a boil.
3. Add the pork belly to the pot, cover, and lower the heat to a simmer. Cook for 1 hour, turning the pork every 15 minutes.
4. After 1 hour, uncover the pot and simmer for 30 minutes more, turning the pork twice.
5. Remove the pork belly from the pot, cool slightly, and transfer to a zip-top bag. Refrigerate overnight.

6. To serve, slice the pork into ¼-inch pieces and reheat in a skillet with the reduced sauce for 1 to 2 minutes before adding to the ramen bowls. You can strain, save, and use the remaining sauce for preparing more chashu or marinating Ajitama Eggs (page 52).

Mix it up: Add 1 teaspoon of spicy sesame oil to the sauce while braising the pork for an extra kick. If you can't find pork belly, you can substitute pork butt or shoulder. Use the fattiest portion.

Cooking tip: To make this a one-pot meal, use the large stockpot to sear the pork belly. You can use a pressure cooker to speed up the process: Cook the pork in the sauce for 20 minutes on the highest pressure. Release the steam. Turn the pork over, and cook for 20 minutes more on the highest pressure.

CHICKEN KARAAGE

Makes about 12 pieces   Prep time: 15 minutes / Cook time: 5 minutes

Think of this topping as the Japanese version of Southern-fried popcorn chicken. Pronounced *ka-ra-ah-ge*, it was first made in Kyushu, Japan's southernmost region. These bite-size pieces of marinated, breaded, deep-fried chicken thighs are a great crunchy contrast while slurping noodles.

1 tablespoon (1-inch piece) fresh ginger, unpeeled, crushed and chopped

1 garlic clove, crushed and chopped

1 tablespoon sake

1 tablespoon tamari

1 tablespoon dark brown sugar, packed

1 pound boneless, skinless chicken thighs, cut into bite-size pieces

¼ cup potato starch or cornstarch

Vegetable oil, for frying

1. In a large bowl, combine the ginger, garlic, sake, tamari, and brown sugar. Add the chicken pieces and marinate for at least 10 minutes, or overnight, in the refrigerator.

2. Remove the chicken from the marinade and set aside.

3. Place the potato starch on a small plate and dredge the chicken through it twice, letting the pieces sit for 2 minutes between dredgings.

4. Heat 1 inch of vegetable oil to 350°F in a deep skillet or wok over high heat and fry the chicken until golden brown on both sides, about 5 minutes.

5. The chicken pieces can go directly from the skillet to the serving bowls.

Prep tip: If you use chicken breasts, you'll want to flatten them with a mallet or the back edge of a cleaver before cutting into bite-size pieces.

AJITAMA EGGS

These marinated lightly hard-boiled eggs are a favorite ramen topping, right up there with Chashu Pork (page 48). The eggs are boiled to the point where the whites are slightly firm and the yolks are a creamy, custard consistency. Before being sliced in half they are marinated in soy sauce and mirin, or the chashu marinade (see page 48). One egg is standard per bowl, but I like to add two to mine!

3 cups water

4 large eggs, at
   room temperature

3 cups ice water

1 cup soy sauce

¼ cup mirin

2 tablespoons dark brown
   sugar, packed

1. In a medium pot over high heat, bring enough water to cover the eggs by 1 inch to a boil.

2. Gently lower the eggs into the boiling water and cook for 5 to 9 minutes, depending on the size of the eggs.

3. Remove the eggs and immediately put them into a bowl with the ice water to stop the cooking process.

4. In a medium bowl, combine the soy sauce, mirin, and brown sugar. Once cooled, peel the eggs and marinate them in the soy sauce mixture. Cover the bowl with a paper towel; refrigerate overnight.

5. Halve the eggs before adding to the ramen bowls.

Prep tip: You can center the yolks in the raw eggs by rolling them in your palms for 30 seconds before boiling. Older eggs are easier to peel than fresher eggs. You can also use different-size eggs such as quail (boil for 4 minutes) or duck (9 minutes).

LA-YU CHILI OIL

Makes about ¾ cup	Prep time: 10 minutes / Cook time: 10 minutes

This is a common condiment for adding some heat to a dish. You can buy it in most grocery stores, Asian markets, and online. Or you can make your own and customize it to your taste.

½ cup neutral-flavored oil (such as canola, vegetable, peanut, or avocado)

2 garlic cloves, crushed and chopped

1 tablespoon (1-inch piece) fresh ginger, unpeeled, crushed, and chopped

1 scallion, green and white parts, roughly chopped

1 tablespoon red chili flakes or ¼ cup chopped fresh hot peppers

¼ cup toasted sesame oil

1. In a saucepan over medium heat, combine the neutral oil, garlic, ginger, scallion, and red chili flakes. Cook, stirring frequently, for 10 minutes.

2. Remove the saucepan from the heat and stir in the sesame oil. Cool to room temperature before straining the oil into an airtight container. Discard the solids.

Mix it up: Change the proportion of aromatics and peppers to match your need for heat. You can also add other spices and aromatics such as anise, fennel, or coriander. For a touch of umami, add some truffle oil.

Storage tip: Homemade oil lasts in the refrigerator for up to 3 months. The oil may thicken or become cloudy, but will clarify when it returns to room temperature. If you plan to consume the oil quickly, you can store it in a dark cupboard.

MAYU (BLACK GARLIC PASTE)

Makes ¾ cup   **Prep time: 5 minutes / Cook time: 15 minutes**

This simple ramen condiment is made by carefully browning crushed fresh garlic until it turns almost black, but doesn't actually burn. Mayu has a bitter taste. But when a small amount is mixed into ramen or tare and combines with the other flavors, it imparts a nice garlicky flavor. Although it is referred to as blackened garlic paste, mayu should not be confused with blackened garlic, which is garlic that has been fermented.

¼ cup vegetable oil	1 tablespoon (1-inch piece)	¼ cup toasted sesame oil
10 garlic cloves, crushed and chopped	fresh ginger, unpeeled, crushed, and chopped	2 tablespoons soy sauce or tamari

1. In a medium saucepan over medium heat, combine the vegetable oil, garlic, and ginger. Sauté until the garlic begins to turn light brown, stirring occasionally to ensure even browning.
2. Reduce the heat to low and cook until the garlic turns dark brown, about 15 minutes.
3. Remove from the heat and stir in the sesame oil and soy sauce.
4. Transfer to an airtight container and refrigerate for up to 3 months.

Mix it up: For some heat, you can substitute spicy sesame oil for the toasted sesame oil. For added umami, add 1 tablespoon of truffle oil or mushroom powder at the end.

Cooking tip: Keep a close eye on how long you allow the garlic to cook once it turns dark brown. Light charring is good and will add sweetness as its natural sugars caramelize. If you go too far and burn the sugars, the result is a bitter taste.

VEGETABLE MISO, PAGE 60

FOUR

MISO RAMEN

Miso is one of the oldest ingredients in Japan's culinary history. Miso ramen, however, is one of its newer recipes. It was invented around 1955 in Sapporo, Hokkaido's largest city in northern Japan. Miso is a hearty ramen, fitting well with Sapporo's cold, Siberian winters.

There are several types of miso with different flavors, depending on the type of grain used. The mildest is white or sweet miso, combining rice and soybeans. Next is yellow miso, which uses a combination of rice, barley, or wheat. Red miso has the strongest flavor, with a mixture of soybeans and barley, and is fermented for up to three years.

Miso ramen toppings tend to be hearty to help diners face long, cold winters. Pork, chicken, beef, and seafood are all favorites. Thick, cloudy kotteri-style broths and strong or spicy tares also fortify against the cold winter air and water currents that come from nearby Siberia.

TOFU MISO

Makes 4 bowls   **Prep time: 15 minutes / Cook time: 10 minutes**

Vegan ramen soups do not have the robust umami flavor associated with broths made from boiling bones or dried fish. However, this recipe combines all the sources of plant-based umami into one bowl. You don't have to be a vegan to enjoy it!

½ cup Miso Tare (page 41)

6 cups Vegan Broth
  (page 40)

1 ounce dried shiitake
  mushrooms, sliced

¼ cup vegetable oil

1 pound extra-firm tofu, cut
  into ½-inch cubes, drained
  and patted dry

3 garlic cloves, crushed
  and chopped

1 tablespoon (1-inch piece)
  fresh ginger, unpeeled,
  crushed and chopped

1 pound fresh or Homemade
  Ramen Noodles
  (page 46), **or 8 ounces
  dried noodles**

¼ cup sliced scallion, green
  and white parts

½ cup sweet corn

1 cup bean sprouts

1 sheet nori, cut into
  3-by-½-inch strips

1. Spoon 2 tablespoons of tare into each serving bowl.

2. In a saucepan over medium heat, bring the broth and mushrooms to a simmer.

3. Remove the rehydrated mushrooms from the broth and divide them among the bowls.

4. Heat the oil in a large skillet over medium-high heat and stir-fry the tofu for about 5 minutes until it begins to turn light brown. Add the garlic and ginger and continue stir-frying until the aromatics are lightly charred and the tofu is golden brown.

5. Distribute the fried tofu among the bowls.

6. Bring a large stockpot full of water to a boil over high heat. Add the noodles and boil (1 minute for fresh, 3 to 4 minutes for dry), then drain.

7. Just before the noodles are done, ladle the broth into the bowls. Add the noodles to each bowl and stir gently, mixing the tare, broth, and noodles.

8. Top the bowls with the scallion, corn, bean sprouts, and nori strips.

9. Serve immediately.

Prep tip: If you want firmer tofu, drain and freeze it. Once it thaws, you'll see it looks like a sponge and is much firmer. You can also press tofu between two plates to drain the liquid, which helps it fry up and absorb more flavor.

Make it simpler: Use your favorite vegetarian or vegan bouillon or broth in place of the vegan broth.

VEGETABLE MISO

Makes 4 bowls   **Prep time: 15 minutes / Cook time: 10 minutes**

This vegan miso ramen features pungent mayu (black garlic paste) paired with the mild bite of Japanese shishito peppers. *Shishito* means "lion's head" in Japanese, as the tip of the pepper is said to resemble the animal. Although shishito peppers are mild, about 1 in 10 is very hot. Someone might get a surprise in their bowl!

½ cup Miso Tare (page 41)

4 teaspoons Mayu (page 54)

6 cups Vegan Broth (page 40)

1 ounce dried shiitake mushrooms, sliced

1 pound silken tofu, cut into 1-inch cubes

8 shishito peppers, seeded and cut into ⅛-inch circles

1 pound fresh or Homemade Ramen Noodles (page 46), **or 8 ounces dried noodles**

¼ cup sliced scallion, green and white parts

4 teaspoons wakame

1. Spoon 2 tablespoons of tare into each serving bowl.
2. Spoon 1 teaspoon of mayu into each bowl.
3. In a large saucepan over medium heat, bring the broth and mushrooms to a simmer.
4. Remove the rehydrated mushrooms from the broth and divide them among the bowls along with the tofu and peppers.

5. Bring a large stockpot full of water to a boil over high heat. Add the noodles and boil (1 minute for fresh, 3 to 4 minutes for dry), then drain.

6. Just before the noodles are done, ladle the broth into the bowls. Add the noodles to each bowl and stir gently, mixing the noodles, tare, mayu, and broth.

7. Top the bowls with the scallion and wakame.

8. Serve immediately.

Variation: Coconut Kare. Give this ramen bowl some curry flavor by adding ½ cup Kare (Curry) Coconut Tare (page 44) along with the miso tare.

PEANUT MISO

Makes 4 bowls   Prep time: 15 minutes / Cook time: 10 minutes

The addition of peanut butter adds a creamy texture to this vegetarian dish. When you first taste the broth, the savory flavor will be immediately evident. The peanut aroma combines with the nutty taste of the sesame oil. The chili peppers will wake up your taste buds for the next slurp.

½ cup Miso Tare (page 41)

6 cups Vegan Broth
   (page 40)

1 ounce dried shiitake
   mushrooms, sliced

¼ cup peanut butter

1 teaspoon spicy sesame oil

1 pound fresh or Homemade
   Ramen Noodles
   (page 46), or 8 ounces
   dried noodles

4 Ajitama Eggs (page 52),
   halved lengthwise

¼ cup sliced scallion, green
   and white parts

½ cup sweet corn

1. Spoon 2 tablespoons of tare into each serving bowl.

2. In a large saucepan over medium heat, bring the broth and mushrooms to a simmer.

3. Remove the rehydrated mushrooms from the broth and divide them among the bowls.

4. Stir the peanut butter and spicy sesame oil into the broth.

5. Bring a large stockpot full of water to a boil over high heat. Add the noodles and boil (1 minute for fresh, 3 to 4 minutes for dry), then drain.

6. Just before the noodles are done, ladle the broth into the bowls. Add the noodles to each bowl and stir gently, mixing the noodles, tare, and broth.

7. Float 2 egg halves in each bowl, and top with the scallion and corn.

8. Serve immediately.

Variation: Pistachio Miso. Swap the peanut butter for pistachio butter. Make your own pistachio butter by grinding ½ cup shelled nuts in a food processor, or buy it premade online. Cashew, macadamia, or almond butter also works well here.

SAPPORO SEAFOOD MISO

Makes 4 bowls   **Prep time: 15 minutes / Cook time: 10 minutes**

This recipe was invented in Sapporo, on Japan's northernmost island of Hokkaido. The flavorful miso and creamy tonkotsu-based broth is filled with umami. Shrimp, corn, bean sprouts, and butter provide protein and fat to help face long winters.

½ cup **Miso Tare** (page 41)

6 cups **Tonkotsu Pork Broth** (page 38)

12 **medium shrimp, shelled, deveined, and halved lengthwise**

1 pound **fresh or Homemade Ramen Noodles** (page 46), **or 8 ounces dried noodles**

4 tablespoons (½ stick) **butter**

¼ cup **sliced scallion, green and white parts**

½ cup **bean sprouts**

½ cup **sweet corn**

4 **Ajitama Eggs** (page 52), **halved lengthwise**

1 sheet **nori, cut into 3-by-½-inch strips**

1. Spoon 2 tablespoons of tare into each serving bowl.

2. In a large saucepan over medium heat, bring the broth to a simmer.

3. Add the shrimp to the broth and cook until they curl and turn opaque, about 2 minutes. Remove the shrimp and set aside.

4. Bring a large stockpot full of water to a boil over high heat. Add the noodles and boil (1 minute for fresh, 3 to 4 minutes for dry), then drain.

5. Just before the noodles are done, ladle the broth into the bowls. Add the noodles to each bowl and stir gently, mixing the tare and broth.

6. Place 1 tablespoon of butter on top of the noodles in each bowl.

7. Top the bowls with the shrimp, scallion, bean sprouts, and corn. Float 2 egg halves in each bowl, and top with the nori strips.

8. Serve immediately.

Variation: Scallop Miso. Swap the shrimp for 1 pound of sea scallops or white fish such as haddock or cod fillets cut into bite-size pieces. Poach until just opaque, about 2 minutes.

Make it simpler: A quick miso tare can be made by mixing equal parts miso and your favorite barbecue sauce. No need to cook it.

CHICKEN MISO

Makes 4 bowls   **Prep time: 15 minutes / Cook time: 10 minutes**

Chicken karaage was developed in the 1920s. The crispy, juicy, marinated fried chicken contrasts with the rich chicken broth and moist chewy noodles. Sweet crunchy bean sprouts pair nicely with the smooth saltiness of the ajitama eggs.

½ cup Miso Tare (page 41)

6 cups Cloudy Chicken
   Broth (page 36)

12 pieces Chicken Karaage
   (page 50)

1 pound fresh or Homemade
   Ramen Noodles

(page 46), **or 8 ounces
   dried noodles**

**Toasted or spicy sesame oil,
   for drizzling on chicken**

¼ cup sliced scallion, green
   and white parts

½ cup sweet corn

½ cup bean sprouts

4 Ajitama Eggs (page 52),
   halved lengthwise

1 sheet nori, cut into
   3-by-½-inch strips

1. Spoon 2 tablespoons of tare into each serving bowl.

2. In a large saucepan over medium heat, bring the broth to a simmer.

3. Meanwhile, in a large dry skillet over medium heat, reheat the chicken karaage, about 3 minutes. Keep warm in the pan until ready to serve.

4. Bring a large stockpot full of water to a boil over high heat. Add the noodles and boil (1 minute for fresh, 3 to 4 minutes for dry), then drain.

5. Just before the noodles are done, ladle the broth into the bowls. Add the noodles to each bowl and stir gently, mixing the tare and broth.

6. Place 3 pieces of chicken into each bowl and drizzle with sesame oil.
7. Top each bowl with the scallion, corn, and bean sprouts. Float 2 egg halves in each bowl. Distribute the nori strips among the bowls.
8. Serve immediately.

Variation: Pork Tenderloin Miso. Change up the protein by substituting pork tenderloin for the chicken thighs in the karaage recipe.

Make it simpler: You can skip the breading and stir-fry the marinated chicken in a couple of tablespoons of vegetable oil.

GROUND PORK MISO

Makes 4 bowls   **Prep time: 15 minutes / Cook time: 10 minutes**

If you want the flavor of chashu but don't have any braised pork belly handy, this quick version using ground pork cooked right in the rich tonkotsu broth provides an excellent and fast alternative. Make sure to buy sausage-grade ground pork, as it has more fat, and hence, more flavor.

½ cup Miso Tare (page 41)

6 cups Tonkotsu Pork Broth (page 38)

4 ounces fresh shiitake mushrooms, sliced

1 pound sausage-grade ground pork

1 pound fresh or Homemade Ramen Noodles (page 46), **or 8 ounces dried noodles**

¼ cup sliced scallion, green and white parts

½ cup bean sprouts

4 Ajitama Eggs (page 52), halved lengthwise

1 sheet nori, cut into 3-by-½-inch strips

1. Spoon 2 tablespoons of tare into each serving bowl.
2. In a large saucepan over medium heat, bring the broth and mushrooms to a simmer.
3. Remove the mushrooms from the broth and divide them among the bowls.
4. Crumble the ground pork into bite-size chunks and add the pieces to the broth.
5. Bring a large stockpot full of water to a boil over high heat. Add the noodles and boil (1 minute for fresh, 3 to 4 minutes for dry), then drain.

6. Just before the noodles are done, ladle the broth into the bowls. (It's fine if some pork makes it into the bowl at this point as well.) Add the noodles to each bowl and stir gently, mixing the noodles, tare, and broth.

7. Distribute the remaining cooked pork among the bowls.

8. Top each bowl with the scallion and bean sprouts. Float 2 egg halves in each bowl. Distribute the nori strips among the bowls.

9. Serve immediately.

Variation: Shaved Beef Miso. Use shaved beef (1 pound rib eye) instead of pork, which will cook up in a matter of seconds in the simmering broth. You can also substitute other ground, chopped, or thinly sliced meat.

AKAYU MISO KAMABOKO

Makes 4 bowls   **Prep time: 15 minutes / Cook time: 10 minutes**

Akayu ramen was invented in 1960 by Sato Kazumi, the owner of a ramen shop in Honshu, Japan. He had some leftover mild miso ramen soup and spiced it up with a paste of miso, hot chili oil, and garlic. The paste is not mixed in or eaten alone. Instead, the noodles are lightly dipped into the spicy paste with chopsticks before being slurped.

8 (¼-inch-thick) slices
  Chashu Pork (page 48)
⅓ cup **Miso Tare** (page 41)
2 tablespoons **La-Yu Chili
  Oil** (page 53)
1 tablespoon
  cayenne pepper

2 tablespoons **Mayu**
  (page 54)
6 cups **Fish Broth** (page 37)
1 pound fresh or **Homemade
  Ramen Noodles**
  (page 46), **or 8 ounces
  dried noodles**

6 ounces **kamaboko
  (steamed fish cake), cut
  into 8 disks**
¼ cup sliced scallion, green
  and white parts
1 (8-ounce) can bamboo
  shoots, drained and rinsed
4 teaspoons wakame

1. In a dry skillet over medium-high heat, sear the chashu on both sides until light golden brown, about 3 minutes. Set aside.
2. In a small bowl, combine the tare, chili oil, cayenne, and mayu.
3. In a large saucepan over medium heat, bring the broth to a simmer.

Continued >>

4. Bring a large stockpot full of water to a boil over high heat. Add the noodles and boil (1 minute for fresh, 3 to 4 minutes for dry), then drain.

5. Just before the noodles are done cooking, ladle the broth into the bowls, and add the noodles.

6. Add 2 tablespoons of the prepared spicy miso tare to each bowl.

7. Add the chashu and kamaboko.

8. Top each bowl with the scallion and bamboo shoots, and sprinkle with the wakame.

9. Serve immediately.

Variation: Additional Assari Broth Flavors. You can change up the flavor of this bowl by substituting another clear assari broth such as Clear Chicken Broth (page 34) or Vegan Broth (page 40).

Prep tip: If you can't get kamaboko, you can substitute artificial crab legs.

TERIYAKI CHICKEN AND SALMON SHIO, PAGE 82

FIVE

SHIO RAMEN

Shio or salt ramen is the original and oldest of the four main types of ramen. In addition to the flavor of salt, shio also derives flavor from chicken, pork, beef, fish, and such vegetarian sources as konbu, miso, and mushrooms. Shio broths are light assari-style broths. When bones are used they are simmered rather than boiled vigorously to minimize emulsification and cloudiness. Shio ramen can be simple and it can be complex. This is because salt, its main source of flavor, also enhances other flavors. A simple shio broth of chicken and salt is pretty straightforward. The salt brings out the chicken flavor. A shio broth that consists of a number of ingredients such as mushrooms, konbu, and dashi would require careful balancing of the salt and umami flavors given to the broth from each of the components. That would be a fun and tasty challenge!

VEGAN KARE SHIO

Makes 4 bowls   **Prep time: 15 minutes / Cook time: 10 minutes**

This shio has a coconut curry kick. It combines shio, the oldest ramen tare, with kare, one of the newest. Coconut combines with the curry in a couple of ways. First, its sweetness helps the different areas of your tongue taste the curry flavors. Second, coconut milk has a significant amount of fat, which helps carry the flavors of the ramen even further.

½ cup Shio Tare (page 42)

½ cup Kare (Curry) Coconut Tare (page 44)

4 cups Vegan Broth (page 40)

1 ounce dried shiitake mushrooms, sliced

1 pound silken tofu, cut into 1-inch squares

16 snow or sugar snap pea pods

4 shishito peppers, seeded and cut into ⅛-inch circles

1 pound fresh or Homemade Ramen Noodles (page 46), or 8 ounces dried noodles

¼ cup sliced scallion, green and white parts

1 sheet nori, cut into 3-by-½-inch strips

1. Spoon 2 tablespoons of shio tare into each serving bowl.
2. Spoon 2 tablespoons of coconut tare into each serving bowl.
3. In a large saucepan over high heat, bring the broth and mushrooms to a simmer.
4. Remove the rehydrated mushrooms from the broth and distribute them among the bowls.

5. Distribute the tofu, pea pods, and peppers among the bowls.

6. Bring a large stockpot full of water to a boil over high heat. Add the noodles and boil (1 minute for fresh, 3 to 4 minutes for dry), then drain.

7. Just before the noodles are done, ladle the broth into the bowls. Add the noodles to each bowl and stir gently, mixing the noodles, tare, vegetables, and broth.

8. Top each bowl with the scallion and nori strips.

9. Serve immediately.

Variation: Hot and Sour Ramen. Add 1 tablespoon of spicy sesame oil and ¼ cup of rice vinegar to the vegan broth to amp up the curry kick in the kare tare.

SEAFOOD SHIO

Makes 4 bowls   Prep time: 15 minutes / Cook time: 10 minutes

The simplicity of the shio-based broth embraces the sweet and savory flavors of the dashi (fish broth) and mushrooms. The salt and the lemon bring pops of acidity while the shrimp and fish lightly poached in the broth bring a hint of sweetness.

1 cup Shio Tare (page 42)

2 cups Fish Broth (page 37)

Juice of 1 lemon

Zest of 1 lemon

1 ounce fresh shiitake
  mushrooms, sliced

8 ounces white flaky
  fish, (cod, haddock,
  or sea bass), cut into
  1-inch pieces

8 ounces medium shrimp,
  peeled, deveined, and
  halved lengthwise

1 pound fresh or Homemade
  Ramen Noodles
  (page 46), or 8 ounces
  dried noodles

16 snow or sugar snap
  pea pods

4 Ajitama Eggs (page 52),
  halved lengthwise

¼ cup sliced scallion, green
  and white parts

1 sheet nori, cut into
  3-by-½-inch strips

1. Spoon ¼ cup of tare into each serving bowl.

2. In a large saucepan over high heat, bring the broth, lemon juice and zest, and mushrooms to a simmer.

3. Add the fish and shrimp to the simmering broth and cook until the shrimp curl and the fish is opaque, about 2 minutes. Remove the mushrooms, shrimp, and fish from the broth and set aside.

4. Bring a large stockpot full of water to a boil over high heat. Add the noodles and boil (1 minute for fresh, 3 to 4 minutes for dry), then drain.

5. Just before the noodles are done, ladle the broth into the bowls. Add the noodles to each bowl and stir gently, mixing the noodles, tare, and broth.

6. Top the bowls with the shrimp, fish, mushrooms, and pea pods.

7. Float 2 egg halves in each bowl, and top with the scallion and nori strips.

8. Serve immediately.

Variation: Scallops and Squid Shio. Swap the fish and shrimp for fresh sea scallops and squid. You can tell scallops are cooked when the edges have just begun to crack and the center is darker than the edges. It's okay if they are a little underdone because they will continue to cook in the broth. When purchasing cleaned and cut-up squid, be sure to include the tentacles. They are the best indicator of when the squid is cooked. As soon as the tentacles curl the squid is done. If you leave them in more than 30 seconds after they have curled they get rubbery.

OSAKA SHIO

Makes 4 bowls   **Prep time: 15 minutes / Cook time: 10 minutes**

Osaka is one of Japan's largest port cities. It is also recognized internationally for its restaurants and food culture. In honor of the city, this shio-based ramen is surf-and-turf-style, with braised chashu pork and seafood.

1 cup Shio Tare (page 42)

4 cups Cloudy Chicken Broth (page 36)

8 medium shrimp, shelled, deveined, and halved lengthwise

8 large sea scallops, halved lengthwise

8 (¼-inch-thick) slices Chashu Pork (page 48)

1 pound fresh or Homemade Ramen Noodles (page 46), **or 8 ounces dried noodles**

4 (¼-inch-thick) slices kamaboko (steamed fish cake)

4 Ajitama Eggs (page 52), halved lengthwise

¼ cup sliced scallion, green and white parts

1 sheet nori, cut into 3-by-½-inch strips

1. Spoon ¼ cup of tare into each serving bowl.
2. In a large saucepan over medium heat, bring the broth to a simmer.
3. Add the shrimp and scallops to the broth. Remove the scallops as soon as the edges begin to crack, and the shrimp when they have curled, about 2 minutes. Set aside.
4. In a large dry skillet over medium-high heat, sear the chashu on both sides, about 3 minutes, until light golden brown. Set aside.
5. Bring a large stockpot full of water to a boil over high heat. Add the noodles and boil (1 minute for fresh, 3 to 4 minutes for dry), then drain.

6. Just before the noodles are done, ladle the broth into each bowl. Add the noodles to each bowl and stir gently, mixing the noodles, tare, and broth.

7. Add the kamaboko, scallops, shrimp, and chashu to the bowls.

8. Float 2 egg halves in each bowl and top with the scallion and nori strips.

9. Serve immediately.

Variation: Steak and Seafood Shio. Instead of the chashu, use 8 ounces shaved steak marinated in 2 tablespoons soy sauce, 2 tablespoons sake, and 2 tablespoons dark brown sugar. Dredge the steak through the boiling broth to cook it before placing it into the bowls.

Prep tip: If possible, use only fresh "dry" sea scallops that have not been previously frozen or treated with salt water. Scallops lose their sweetness when frozen and thawed. Some vendors soak scallops in a brine to keep them plumped up, altering flavor and texture.

TERIYAKI CHICKEN AND SALMON SHIO

Makes 4 bowls   **Prep time: 15 minutes / Cook time: 10 minutes**

Teriyaki means "shining grill," and refers to the glaze that forms when food is marinated and then grilled, roasted, or stir-fried. In Japan, teriyaki is most often used to cook fish, while in the United States, chicken is more popular. This recipe combines these two favorites for the best of both worlds.

1 cup Shio Tare (page 42)

2 cups Fish Broth (page 37)

2 cups Clear Chicken Broth (page 34)

1 ounce dried shiitake mushrooms, sliced

1 garlic clove, crushed and chopped

1 tablespoon (1-inch piece) fresh ginger, unpeeled, crushed and chopped

1 tablespoon honey

I tablespoon soy sauce

1 tablespoon mirin

8 ounces boneless chicken thighs, cut into bite-size pieces

8 ounces salmon fillet, whole or cut into bite-size pieces

2 tablespoons vegetable oil, divided

24 snow or sugar snap pea pods

1 pound fresh or Homemade Ramen Noodles (page 46), **or 8 ounces dried noodles**

¼ cup sliced scallion, green and white parts

1 sheet nori, cut into 3-by-½-inch strips

1. Spoon ¼ cup of tare into each serving bowl.

2. In a large saucepan over high heat, bring the fish broth, chicken broth, and mushrooms to a simmer.

3. Remove the rehydrated mushrooms from the broth and divide among the bowls.

4. In a large bowl, combine the garlic, ginger, honey, soy sauce, and mirin; divide the mixture between two bowls. Add the chicken and salmon pieces in the separate bowls and marinate for 5 minutes. If using a whole piece of salmon, marinate at room temperature for 20 minutes.

5. Heat 1 tablespoon of oil in a large skillet over high heat. When it just begins to smoke, add the chicken and stir-fry for about 5 minutes, until lightly brown and crispy. Remove and set aside.

6. Add the remaining 1 tablespoon of oil to the skillet and stir-fry the salmon for about 3 minutes, until lightly brown and crispy. Remove and set aside.

7. Distribute the pea pods among the bowls.

8. Bring a large stockpot full of water to a boil over high heat. Add the noodles and boil (1 minute for fresh, 3 to 4 minutes for dry), then drain.

9. Just before the noodles are done, ladle the broth into the bowls. Add the noodles to each bowl and stir gently, mixing the noodles, pea pods, tare, and broth.

10. To each bowl, add the chicken and salmon and top with the scallion and nori strips.

11. Serve immediately.

Variation: Sweet and Sour Shio. Add 1 tablespoon cornstarch, 2 tablespoons dark brown sugar, and ¼ cup rice vinegar to the chicken in step 4 and stir-fry for 2 more minutes until a glaze forms. Remove the chicken and half the glaze.

KYOTO SHIO

Makes 4 bowls   **Prep time: 15 minutes / Cook time: 10 minutes**

Although the ramen chefs in Hakodate (where shio ramen is a specialty) will no doubt disagree, Kyoto is recognized as having some of the best shio ramen in Japan. The combination of rich tonkotsu broth and salty shio tare enhances the umami flavors of the toppings.

1 cup Shio Tare (page 42)

4 cups Tonkotsu Pork Broth (page 38)

1 ounce dried shiitake mushrooms, sliced

8 (¼-inch-thick) slices Chashu Pork (page 48)

16 snow or sugar snap pea pods

1 pound fresh or Homemade Ramen Noodles (page 46), **or 8 ounces dried noodles**

4 Ajitama Eggs (page 52), halved lengthwise

¼ cup sliced scallion, green and white parts

1. Spoon ¼ cup of tare into each serving bowl.
2. In a large saucepan over high heat, bring the broth and mushrooms to a simmer.
3. Remove the rehydrated mushrooms from the broth and divide among the bowls.
4. In a large dry skillet over medium-high heat, sear the chashu on both sides, about 3 minutes, until light golden brown. Set aside.

5. Distribute the pea pods among the bowls.

6. Bring a large stockpot full of water to a boil over high heat. Add the noodles and boil (1 minute for fresh, 3 to 4 minutes for dry), then drain.

7. Just before the noodles are done, ladle the broth into the bowls. Add the noodles to each bowl and stir gently, mixing the noodles, tare, pea pods, and broth.

8. Float 2 egg halves in each bowl and top with the chashu and scallion. Serve immediately.

Variations: Fried Ham Ramen. A tasty variation is to quickly prepare some stir-fried meat noodles. Take 8 ounces thinly sliced deli ham and cut into ¼- to ⅛-inch noodles. Toss the ham into a dry skillet and stir-fry the "noodles" for 2 to 3 minutes. There's no need to add any oil. As the "noodles" sear they will smell great and add some tasty texture to the bowl.

HAKODATE SHIO

Makes 4 bowls   **Prep time: 15 minutes / Cook time: 10 minutes**

Hakodate was the first Japanese seaport open to international trade. Chinese merchants brought noodles, leading to the first noodle houses, eventually becoming ramen houses, or ramen-ya. Salt and konbu are readily available in Hakodate, making shio ramen infused with konbu a specialty.

1 cup **Shio Tare** (page 42)

6 cups **Clear Chicken Broth** (page 34)

8 (¼-inch-thick) slices **Chashu Pork** (page 48)

1 pound fresh or **Homemade Ramen Noodles**

(page 46)**, or 8 ounces dried noodles**

4 (¼-inch-thick) slices **kamaboko (steamed fish cake)**

4 **Ajitama Eggs** (page 52), **halved lengthwise**

¼ cup **sliced scallion, green and white parts**

1 cup **bean sprouts**

4 teaspoons **wakame**

1. Place ¼ cup of tare into each serving bowl.
2. In a large saucepan over medium heat, bring the broth to a simmer.
3. In a large dry skillet over medium-high heat, sear the chashu on each side, about 3 minutes, until light golden brown. Set aside.
4. Bring a large stockpot full of water to a boil over high heat. Add the noodles and boil (1 minute for fresh, 3 to 4 minutes for dry), then drain.

5. Just before the noodles are done, ladle the broth into the bowls. Add the noodles to each bowl and stir gently, mixing the noodles, tare, and broth.

6. Top the bowls with the chashu, kamaboko, 2 egg halves, scallion, bean sprouts, and wakame.

7. Serve immediately.

Variation: Alternative Broths. Substitute another clear broth, such as Fish Broth (page 37) or Vegan Broth (page 40) for the chicken broth in this recipe.

Make it simpler: Use canned broth or bouillon for the broth. When using bouillon, make it half strength as it's usually too strong for ramen broth, given the addition of tare.

SHAVED BEEF SHIO

Makes 4 bowls   **Prep time: 15 minutes / Cook time: 10 minutes**

This hearty shio ramen takes advantage of how quickly thinly shaved rib-eye steak cooks in steaming broth. The salty shio tare is perfect for bringing out the umami flavors of the meat.

1 cup **Shio Tare** (page 42)

4 cups **Fish Broth** (page 37)

1 pound **shaved rib-eye steak, at room temperature**

4 **shishito peppers, stemmed and cut into ⅛-inch circles**

24 **snow or sugar snap pea pods**

1 pound **fresh or Homemade Ramen Noodles** (page 46)**, or 8 ounces dried noodles**

½ **cup sweet corn**

¼ **cup sliced scallion, green and white parts**

1 **sheet nori, cut into 3-by-½-inch strips**

1.   Spoon ¼ cup of tare into each serving bowl.

2.   In a large saucepan over medium heat, bring the broth to a simmer.

3.   Distribute the shaved beef among the bowls arranging the meat loosely, separating any clumps.

4.   Distribute the peppers and pea pods among the bowls.

5.   Bring a large stockpot full of water to a boil over high heat. Add the noodles and boil (1 minute for fresh, 3 to 4 minutes for dry), then drain.

Continued >>

6. Just before the noodles are done, ladle the broth into the bowls. Add the noodles to each bowl and stir gently, mixing the noodles, tare, beef, peppers, pea pods, and broth.

7. Top the bowls with the corn, scallion, and nori strips.

8. Serve immediately.

Variation: Marinated Steak Shio. Marinate the steak with 2 tablespoons of your favorite sauce or seasoning before placing it in the bowls.

Prep tip: Take the steak out of the refrigerator about 30 minutes before preparing the ingredients to let it warm up. If the steak is cold it will cool the broth and it may not cook enough.

SUSAKI RAMEN, PAGE 107

SIX

SHOYU RAMEN

Soy sauce was introduced to Japan by Chinese Buddhists in the 7th century. Shoyu is one of the oldest sauces and is likely the earliest vegetarian sauce. It is one of the original and most widely available ramen types across Japan. Shoyu ramen appeared in 1910 at a Tokyo restaurant, Rairaiken, which closed in 1944. An apprentice opened Shinraiken nearby where they continue making the original recipe. Shoyu ramen consists primarily of a clear, assari-style broth, but can also be made with cloudy broths. Noodles tend to be thicker or wider, such as udon and soba noodles. Toppings include chashu, kamaboko, bamboo shoots, and ajitama as well as regional favorites. Regional styles of shoyu ramen result in a variety of ingredients used in the broth to augment the natural umami flavor of fermented soy beans, such as mushrooms, dried seaweed, fish, and miso.

KITAKATA RAMEN

Makes 4 bowls   **Prep time: 15 minutes / Cook time: 10 minutes**

This ramen is named after Kitakata, in central Japan. It originated there in the 1920s, where vendors sold soup with Chinese noodles. Even today, Kitakata ramen is referred to as chuka soba, or Chinese noodles. Although it's a small city by Japanese standards, Kitakata may have the most ramen-ya per capita, with more than 120.

1 cup Shoyu Tare (page 43)

4 cups Tonkotsu Pork Broth (page 38)

8 (¼-inch-thick) slices Chashu Pork (page 48)

1 pound fresh udon noodles, or 8 ounces dried noodles

8 (¼-inch-thick) slices kamaboko (steamed fish cake)

4 ounces menma

¼ cup sliced scallion, green and white parts

1 sheet nori, cut into 3-by-½-inch strips

1. Spoon ¼ cup of tare into each serving bowl.
2. In a large saucepan over medium heat, bring the broth to a simmer.
3. In a large dry skillet over medium-high heat, sear the chashu on both sides, about 3 minutes, until light golden brown. Set aside.
4. Bring a large stockpot full of water to a boil over high heat. Add the noodles and boil (1 minute for fresh, 3 to 4 minutes for dry), then drain.

5. Just before the noodles are done, ladle the broth into the bowls. Add the noodles to each bowl and stir gently, mixing the noodles, tare, and broth.

6. Top the bowls with the chashu, kamaboko, menma, scallion, and nori strips.

7. Serve immediately.

Variation: Tori Paitan. Cloudy Chicken Broth (page 36) can be substituted for the Tonkotsu.

ONOMICHI RAMEN

Makes 4 bowls   Prep time: 15 minutes / Cook time: 10 minutes

Onomichi is a port city on Honshu Island. This ramen is influenced by its proximity to the ocean, where dashi, nori, and kamaboko blend with the sweetness of the chashu. Although it was invented in the 1940s, the style didn't become popular until the 1990s.

1 cup **Shoyu Tare** (page 43)

4 cups **Fish Broth** (page 37)

8 (¼-inch-thick) slices **Chashu Pork** (page 48)

1 pound **fresh udon noodles,** or 8 ounces dried noodles

4 (¼-inch-thick) slices kamaboko (steamed fish cake)

2 **Ajitama Eggs** (page 52), halved lengthwise

¼ cup sliced scallion, green and white parts

4 ounces menma

1 sheet nori, cut into 3-by-½-inch strips

1. Place ¼ cup of tare into each serving bowl.
2. In a large saucepan over medium heat, bring the broth to a simmer.
3. In a large dry skillet over medium-high heat, sear the chashu on both sides, about 3 minutes, until light golden brown. Set aside.
4. Bring a large stockpot full of water to a boil over high heat. Add the noodles and boil (1 minute for fresh, 3 to 4 minutes for dry), then drain.

5. Just before the noodles are done, ladle the broth into the bowls. Add the noodles to each bowl and stir gently, mixing the noodles, tare, and broth.

6. Top the bowls with the kamaboko, half an egg, chashu, scallion, menma, and nori strips.

7. Serve immediately.

Variation: Onomichi Salmon Ramen. Instead of chashu, use 8 ounces salmon marinated for 5 minutes in 2 tablespoons each soy sauce, mirin wine, and honey. Grill or broil and cut into pieces. Or, you can also poach the salmon pieces in the broth for 1 minute before placing them in the bowls.

KASAOKA RAMEN

Makes 4 bowls   **Prep time: 15 minutes / Cook time: 10 minutes**

Kasaoka is located in south coastal Japan in the prefecture of Okayama. This shoyu-based ramen features chicken. The light, assari-style broth provides a flavorful combination of salt and umami with the shoyu tare.

1 cup Shoyu Tare (page 43)

1 pound boneless, skinless chicken thighs, cut into 12 bite-size pieces

2 cups Fish Broth (page 37)

2 cups Clear Chicken Broth (page 34)

1 pound fresh or Homemade Ramen Noodles (page 46), **or 8 ounces dried noodles**

4 (⅛-inch-thick) slices kamaboko (steamed fish cake)

2 Ajitama Eggs (page 52), halved lengthwise

¼ cup sliced scallion, green and white parts

8 ounces menma

1 sheet nori, cut into 3-by-½-inch strips

1. In a large saucepan over medium heat, bring the tare to a simmer, add the chicken, and poach for 3 minutes. Remove the chicken and set aside.

2. Divide the tare among the serving bowls.

3. In the same saucepan, heat the fish broth and chicken broth until the broth comes to a simmer.

4. Bring a large stockpot full of water to a boil over high heat. Add the noodles and boil (1 minute for fresh, 3 to 4 minutes for dry), then drain.

5. Just before the noodles are done, ladle the broth into the bowls. Add the noodles to each bowl and stir gently, mixing the noodles, tare, and broth.
6. Top each bowl with the chicken, kamaboko, half an egg, scallion, menma, and nori strips.
7. Serve immediately.

Variation: Kasaoka Ramen with Chicken Tenders. Use breast meat instead of thighs. I recommend using chicken tenders, which are the thinner part of the breast.

HOKKAIDO RAMEN

Makes 4 bowls   Prep time: 15 minutes / Cook time: 10 minutes

Hokkaido is Japan's northernmost island. Its meaning in Japanese is "northern seaway." This hearty recipe combines pork, ginger, and miso to help the locals withstand Hokkaido's long, cold winters.

1 cup Shoyu Tare (page 43)

1 tablespoon vegetable oil

1 pound ground pork

3 garlic cloves, smashed and chopped

1 tablespoon (1-inch piece) fresh ginger, unpeeled, smashed, and chopped

1 tablespoon dark brown sugar, packed

4 cups Cloudy Chicken Broth (page 36)

¼ cup white or yellow mild miso

1 ounce dried shiitake mushrooms, sliced

1 cup shredded napa cabbage

1 pound fresh or Homemade Ramen Noodles (page 46), or 8 ounces dried noodles

4 tablespoons (½ stick) salted butter, at room temperature

½ cup sliced scallion, green and white parts

½ cup sweet corn

8 ounces menma

1. Spoon ¼ cup of tare into each serving bowl.
2. In a large skillet over medium-high heat, heat the oil and stir-fry the ground pork with the garlic, ginger, and brown sugar until brown, about 5 minutes. Set aside.
3. In a large saucepan over high heat, bring the broth, miso, and mushrooms to a simmer.
4. Remove the rehydrated mushrooms from the broth and divide them among the bowls.
5. Distribute the cabbage among the bowls.

6. Bring a large stockpot full of water to a boil over high heat. Add the noodles and boil (1 minute for fresh, 3 to 4 minutes for dry), then drain.

7. Just before the noodles are done, ladle the broth into the bowls. Add the noodles to each bowl and stir gently, mixing the noodles, tare, vegetables, and broth.

8. Top each bowl with the ground pork, 1 tablespoon of butter, scallion, sweet corn, and menma.

9. Serve immediately.

Variation: Hokkaido Ramen with Greens. Swap the napa cabbage for bok choy, chard, spinach, or kale for a different taste and texture.

Cooking tip: For extra flavor, substitute melted lard (bacon fat) for the butter.

KYOTO RAMEN

Makes 4 bowls   **Prep time: 15 minutes / Cook time: 10 minutes**

Kyoto was the capital of Japan for more than 1,000 years before the capital was changed to Tokyo in 1869. Kyoto is still considered the cultural and religious center of Japan, where there are more than 200 ramen-ya. Kyoto-style ramen favors assari-style chicken broth flavored with shoyu tare. Other toppings that work well with this include chashu, mushrooms, shishito peppers, and scallions. Udon noodles are recommended.

1 cup **Shoyu Tare** (page 43)

4 teaspoons **Mayu** (page 54)

4 cups **Clear Chicken Broth** (page 34)

1 tablespoon **white or yellow mild miso**

1 ounce **dried shiitake mushrooms, sliced**

8 **shishito peppers, seeded and cut into ⅛-inch circles**

8 (¼-inch-thick) slices **Chashu Pork** (page 48)

1 pound fresh or **Homemade Ramen Noodles** (page 46)**, or 8 ounces dried noodles**

½ cup **sliced scallion, green and white parts**

4 tablespoons **salted butter**

½ cup **sweet corn**

1. Spoon ¼ cup of tare and 1 teaspoon of mayu into each serving bowl.

2. In a large saucepan over medium heat, bring the broth, miso, and mushrooms to a simmer.

3. Remove the rehydrated mushrooms from the broth and divide them among the bowls.

4. Distribute the peppers among the bowls.

5. In a large dry skillet over medium-high heat, sear the chashu on both sides, about 3 minutes, until light golden brown. Set aside.

6. Bring a large stockpot full of water to a boil over high heat. Add the noodles and boil (1 minute for fresh, 3 to 4 minutes for dry), then drain.

7. Just before the noodles are done, ladle the broth into the bowls. Add the noodles to each bowl and stir gently, mixing the noodles, tare, vegetables, and broth.

8. Top each bowl with the chashu, scallions, 1 tablespoon of butter, and sweet corn.

9. Serve immediately.

Variation: Tonkotsu Kyoto. Substitute a clear pork bone broth for the chicken broth. Prepare the Tonkotsu Pork Broth (page 38) by simmering rather than boiling. If you use a pressure cooker, the broth will not boil, keeping the broth clear and saving lots of time (3 hours versus 8 hours).

SHIRAKAWA RAMEN

Makes 4 bowls   **Prep time: 15 minutes / Cook time: 10 minutes**

Shirakawa was originally a gated city separating the settled part of Japan from the wild lands to the north. Shirakawa ramen is noted for its buckwheat soba noodles, first served in the 1920s. The clear shoyu-flavored broth pairs well with the sweet chashu, kamaboko, and spinach toppings.

1 cup Shoyu Tare (page 43)

4 cups Clear Chicken Broth
  (page 34)

1 ounce dried shiitake
  mushrooms, sliced

2 cups coarsely chopped
  fresh spinach

8 (¼-inch-thick) slices
  Chashu Pork (page 48)

1 pound fresh soba
  buckwheat noodles, or
  8 ounces dried noodles

4 (¼-inch-thick) slices
  kamaboko (steamed
  fish cake)

½ cup sweet corn

4 tablespoons salted butter

¼ cup sliced scallion, green
  and white parts

1. Spoon ¼ cup of tare into each serving bowl.

2. In a large saucepan over high heat, bring the broth and mushrooms to a simmer.

3. Remove the rehydrated mushrooms from the broth and divide them among the bowls.

4. Distribute the spinach among the bowls.

5. In a large dry skillet over medium-high heat, sear the chashu on both sides, about 3 minutes, until light golden brown. Set aside.

Continued >>

6. Bring a large stockpot full of water to a boil over high heat. Add the noodles and boil (1 minute for fresh, 3 to 4 minutes for dry), then drain.

7. Just before the noodles are done, ladle the broth into the bowls. Add the noodles to each bowl and stir gently, mixing the noodles, tare, vegetables, and broth.

8. Top each bowl with the chashu, kamaboko, corn, 1 tablespoon of butter, and scallion.

9. Serve immediately.

Variation: Vegan Shirakawa. This simple transformation involves swapping Vegan Broth (page 40) for the chicken broth. Heat a couple of tablespoons of oil, miso, Mayu (page 54), and Shoyu Tare (page 43) in a skillet and stir-fry slices of extra-firm tofu (8 ounces) to replace the chashu. Replace the butter with a few dashes of spicy sesame oil.

SUSAKI RAMEN

Makes 4 bowls   **Prep time: 15 minutes / Cook time: 10 minutes**

Susaki-stye ramen is traditionally served in heavy earthenware bowls known as ramen hotpots. The clear chicken base with shoyu tare is usually topped with chicken, scallion, kamaboko, and a raw egg.

1 cup Shoyu Tare (page 43)

4 cups Clear Chicken Broth (page 34)

1 tablespoon miso of your choice

1 ounce dried shiitake mushrooms, sliced

4 large eggs, at room temperature

1 pound fresh or Homemade Ramen Noodles (page 46), **or 8 ounces dried noodles**

8 slices Chicken Karaage (page 50)

8 (¼-inch-thick) slices kamaboko (steamed fish cake)

½ cup sliced scallion, green and white parts

1. Spoon ¼ cup of tare into each serving bowl.
2. In a large saucepan over medium heat, bring the broth, miso, and mushrooms to a simmer.
3. Remove the rehydrated mushrooms from the broth and distribute among the bowls.
4. Gently break 1 egg into each bowl.
5. Bring a large stockpot full of water to a boil over high heat. Add the noodles and boil (1 minute for fresh, 3 to 4 minutes for dry), then drain.

Continued >>

6. Just before the noodles are done, ladle the broth into the bowls. Add the noodles to each bowl and stir gently, mixing the noodles, tare, and broth.

7. Top each bowl with the chicken, kamaboko, and scallion.

8. Serve immediately.

Variation: Poached Egg Susaki. If you are uncomfortable with raw or undercooked eggs you can poach them. Gently break the eggs into a skillet with 1 inch of simmering chicken broth. As they simmer, ladle the broth over them to cook the eggs until they are soft poached.

Cooking tip: The raw or soft-cooked egg yolk is usually stirred into the noodles just before being slurped.

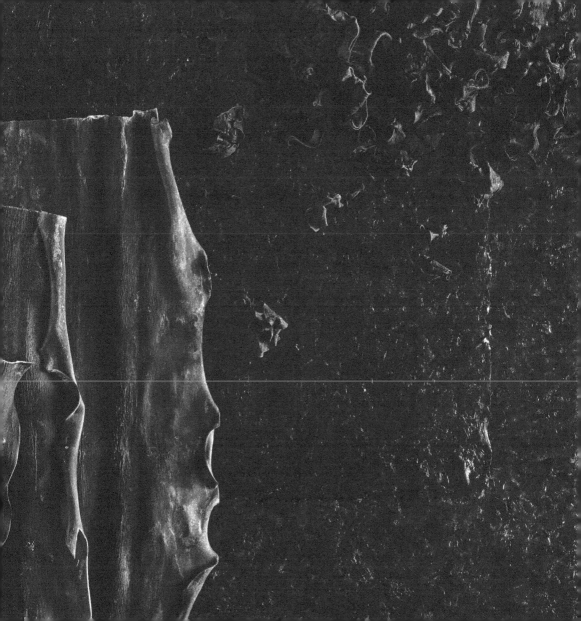

KURUME RAMEN, PAGE 118

SEVEN

TONKOTSU RAMEN

Tonkotsu ramen originated in Kurume on the island of Kyushu. It began as a quick cheap meal for laborers. Boiling pork bones and scraps of meat draws out the flavor from the meat and the collagen protein inside the bones. It also renders the fat, carrying the flavors of garlic, ginger, and scallions in the broth. Although the ingredients and process are simple, the investment of time is significant, 8 to 12 hours, though pressure cookers can reduce this time drastically, as in the master recipe, Tonkotsu Pork Broth (page 38). Prolonged boiling is needed to get the fat and protein in the broth to mix together, or emulsify, so that they don't separate. While tonkotsu can go with everything, the thick, kotteri-style broth pairs best with thinner ramen noodles.

HAKATA RAMEN

Makes 4 bowls   **Prep time: 15 minutes / Cook time: 10 minutes**

Hakata is the business district in the city of Fukuoka, and well known for its tonkotsu ramen. The noodles in Hakata tonkotsu are thin and cook up fast, so workers can eat quickly. Diners can even request the firmness of their noodles. *Barikata* means extra firm. *Kata* is firm. *Futsu* is medium. *Yawa* is soft. And *bariyawa* is extra soft. I recommend barikata.

1 cup Shio Tare (page 42)

4 cups Tonkotsu Pork Broth (page 38)

1 tablespoon miso of your choice

1 ounce dried shiitake mushrooms, sliced

8 (¼-inch-thick) slices Chashu Pork (page 48)

1 pound fresh or Homemade Ramen Noodles (page 46), **or 8 ounces dried noodles**

½ cup sliced scallion, green and white parts

4 ounces pickled ginger

4 garlic cloves, smashed and chopped

4 teaspoons sesame seeds

1. Spoon ¼ cup of tare into each serving bowl.

2. In a large saucepan over medium heat, bring the broth, miso, and mushrooms to a simmer.

3. Remove the rehydrated mushrooms from the broth and divide among the bowls.

4. In a large dry skillet over medium-high heat, sear the chashu on both sides, about 3 minutes, until light golden brown. Set aside.

5. Bring a large stockpot full of water to a boil over high heat. Add the noodles and boil (1 minute for fresh, 3 to 4 minutes for dry), then drain.

6. Just before the noodles are done, ladle the broth into the bowls. Add the noodles to each bowl and stir gently, mixing the noodles, tare, mushrooms, and broth.

7. Top each bowl with the chashu, scallion, pickled ginger, garlic, and 1 teaspoon of sesame seeds.

8. Serve immediately.

Variation: Hakata Shoyu. You can substitute shoyu—or even Miso Tare (page 41)—for the shio. Try topping it with Mayu (page 54) instead of the raw garlic for a less intense flavor profile.

WAKAYAMA RAMEN

Makes 4 bowls	Prep time: 15 minutes / Cook time: 10 minutes

Wakayama is called the holy grail of ramen. This style of ramen is known locally as chuka soba, or Chinese noodles. Ramen is so important in Wakayama, a port city in the southeastern island of Honshu, that tour guides are required to take a test about ramen and its history to earn the title.

1 cup Shoyu Tare (page 43)

4 cups Tonkotsu Pork Broth (page 38)

8 (¼-inch-thick) slices Chashu Pork (page 48)

1 pound fresh or Homemade Ramen Noodles (page 46), **or 8 ounces dried noodles**

2 Ajitama Eggs (page 52), halved lengthwise

4 (¼-inch-thick) slices kamaboko (steamed fish cake)

½ cup sliced scallions, green and white parts

4 ounces menma

1. Spoon ¼ cup of tare into each serving bowl.

2. In a large saucepan over medium heat, bring the broth to a simmer.

3. In a large dry skillet over medium-high heat, sear the chashu on both sides, about 3 minutes, until light golden brown. Set aside

4. Bring a large stockpot full of water to a boil over high heat. Add the noodles and boil (1 minute for fresh, 3 to 4 minutes for dry), then drain.

5. Just before the noodles are done, ladle the broth into the bowls. Add the noodles to each bowl and stir gently, mixing the noodles, tare, and broth.
6. Top each bowl with the chashu, half an egg, kamaboko, scallion, and menma.
7. Serve immediately.

Variation: Kikuni Wakayama. Substitute kikuni for the chashu. Kikuni is pork rib braised the same way as the chashu, except the meat is left on the bone. Ask the butcher to cut the pork ribs in half, making 1- to 2-inch riblets.

OKINAWA SOBA

Makes 4 bowls   Prep time: 15 minutes / Cook time: 10 minutes

The island of Okinawa is known for flavoring its tonkotsu with dashi and konbu. In local ramen-ya, there are pork and seafood toppings, although here I use only pork. Strangely enough, soba noodles are not used in Okinawa soba. In this case, "soba" merely refers to noodles.

1 cup Fish Broth (page 37)

4 cups Tonkotsu Pork Broth (page 38)

1 ounce dried shiitake mushrooms, sliced

8 (¼-inch-thick) slices Chashu Pork (page 48)

1 pound fresh or Homemade Ramen Noodles (page 46), **or 8 ounces dried noodles**

4 (¼-inch-thick) slices kamaboko (steamed fish cake)

2 Ajitama Eggs (page 52), halved lengthwise

½ cup sliced scallion, green and white parts

1 sheet nori, cut into 3-by-½-inch strips

1. In a large saucepan over high heat, bring the fish broth, pork broth, and mushrooms to a simmer.

2. Remove the rehydrated mushrooms from the broth and divide them among the bowls.

3. In a large dry skillet over medium-high heat, sear the chashu on both sides, about 3 minutes, until light golden brown. Set aside.

4. Bring a large stockpot full of water to a boil over high heat. Add the noodles and boil (1 minute for fresh, 3 to 4 minutes for dry), then drain.

5. Just before the noodles are done, ladle the broth into the bowls. Add the noodles to each bowl and stir gently, mixing the noodles, tare, mushrooms, and broth.

6. Top each bowl with the kamaboko, chashu, half an egg, scallion, and nori strips.

7. Serve immediately.

Variation: Seafood Okinawa Soba. Swap the chashu for 8 ounces of seafood, such as shrimp, squid, or scallops. Poach the seafood in the broth and distribute among the bowls just before pouring the broth over the noodles. Don't overcook the seafood when poaching. Squid should be removed from the poaching liquid as soon as the tentacles curl, and scallops are done when the edges begin to crack.

KURUME RAMEN

Makes 4 bowls   **Prep time: 15 minutes / Cook time: 10 minutes**

Kurume was the first tonkotsu-style ramen. It was invented in 1937 at a ramen-ya called Nanjing Senryo, which is still operating today. A cook there mistakenly left a pot of bones boiling overnight. By morning, the broth was milky white and heavy with emulsified collagen and fat, and tonkotsu was born, providing another example of a mistake becoming a culinary discovery!

1 cup Shoyu Tare (page 43)

4 cups Tonkotsu Pork Broth
(page 38)

1 ounce dried shiitake
mushrooms, sliced

8 (¼-inch-thick) slices
Chashu Pork (page 48)

1 pound fresh or Homemade
Ramen Noodles
(page 46), **or 8 ounces
dried noodles**

4 (¼-inch-thick) slices
kamaboko (steamed
fish cake)

4 ounces pickled ginger

½ cup sliced scallion, green
and white parts

2 Ajitama Eggs (page 52),
halved lengthwise

4 teaspoons sesame seeds

1 sheet nori, cut into
3-by-½-inch strips

1. Spoon ¼ cup of tare into each serving bowl.

2. In a medium saucepan over medium heat, bring the broth and mushrooms to a simmer.

3. Remove the rehydrated mushrooms from the broth and divide them among the bowls.

4. In a large dry skillet over medium-high heat, sear the chashu on both sides, about
    3 minutes, until light golden brown. Set aside.

5. Bring a large stockpot full of water to a boil over high heat. Add the noodles and boil (1 minute for fresh, 3 to 4 minutes for dry), then drain.

6. Just before the noodles are done, ladle the broth into the bowls. Add the noodles to each bowl and stir gently, mixing the noodles, tare, mushrooms, and broth.

7. Top each bowl with the chashu, kamaboko, pickled ginger, scallion, half an egg, sesame seeds, and nori strips.

8. Serve immediately.

Variation: Original Kurume Ramen. Go back in time before 1937. Make a clear pork bone broth by simmering rather than boiling Tonkotsu Pork Broth (page 38) and substitute udon noodles.

Cooking tip: Another topping to try with this ramen is spicy mustard greens. You can find them in some grocery stores and most Asian markets. Mustard greens can be used raw, wilted, or parboiled.

KAGOSHIMA RAMEN

Makes 4 bowls   **Prep time: 15 minutes / Cook time: 10 minutes**

Kagoshima's ramen is influenced by its proximity to the ocean. Its tonkotsu broth is typically flavored with miso, wood ear mushrooms, dashi, konbu, and nori. Kagoshima is sometimes referred to as "the Naples of the Eastern World," due to its warm climate, proximity to the ocean, and the presence of Japan's most active stratovolcano, Sakurajima.

1 cup **Fish Broth** (page 37)

4 cups **Tonkotsu Pork Broth** (page 38)

1 ounce **dried wood ear mushrooms, shredded**

4 tablespoons **Miso Tare** (page 41)

8 (¼-inch-thick) slices **Chashu Pork** (page 48)

1 pound fresh or **Homemade Ramen Noodles** (page 46)**, or 8 ounces dried noodles**

4 (¼-inch-thick) slices **kamaboko (steamed fish cake)**

2 **Ajitama Eggs** (page 52)**, halved lengthwise**

½ cup **sliced scallion, green and white parts**

1 cup **bean sprouts**

1 sheet **nori, cut into 3-by-½-inch strips**

1. In a large saucepan over medium heat, bring the fish broth, pork broth, and mushrooms to a simmer.
2. Remove the rehydrated mushrooms from the broth and divide among the serving bowls.
3. Place 1 tablespoon of tare in each bowl.

4. In a large dry skillet over medium-high heat, sear the chashu on both sides, about 3 minutes, until light golden brown. Set aside.

5. Bring a large stockpot full of water to a boil over high heat. Add the noodles and boil (1 minute for fresh, 3 to 4 minutes for dry), then drain.

6. Just before the noodles are done, ladle the broth into the bowls. Add the noodles to each bowl and stir gently, mixing the noodles, tare, mushrooms, and broth.

7. Top each bowl with the chashu, kamaboko, half an egg, scallion, bean sprouts, and nori strips.

8. Serve immediately.

Variation: Kagoshima Kare Ramen. For a less-fishy flavor and more spiciness, substitute 1 cup of Kare (Curry) Coconut Tare (page 44) for the fish broth.

Prep tip: Try shredded daikon radish as a topping, either fresh or pickled. Daikon can be found in some grocery stores and in most Asian markets. It looks like a fat, white carrot and has a mild radish bite to it. Use a peeler to make thin noodle-like strips. To pickle the daikon, place the strips in a jar filled with ½ cup rice or cider vinegar, ½ cup hot water, and ½ cup sugar. Cover and let sit in the refrigerator for at least 2 hours, preferably overnight.

NAGASAKI CHAMPON

Makes 4 bowls   **Prep time: 15 minutes / Cook time: 10 minutes**

Champon is unique to Nagasaki. It might be considered the first ancestor of ramen, as it was first served in 1899, and is based on a Chinese noodle soup recipe. Unlike traditional ramen recipes, champon is a one-pot meal, as the noodles are cooked in the broth, which adds to the richness of the soup.

1 cup **Fish Broth** (page 37)
4 cups **Tonkotsu Pork Broth** (page 38)
1 ounce dried shiitake mushrooms, sliced
1 dozen medium shrimp, peeled, deveined, and halved lengthwise
8 ounces white fish (such as cod or haddock), cut into 1-inch pieces

24 snow peas
8 ounces fresh sea scallops, halved lengthwise
1 pound fresh or **Homemade Ramen Noodles** (page 46), **or 8 ounces dried noodles**
4 (¼-inch-thick) slices kamaboko (steamed fish cake)

½ cup sliced scallion, green and white parts
1 sheet nori, cut into 3-by-½-inch strips

1. In a large saucepan over medium heat, bring the fish broth, pork broth, and mushrooms to a simmer.
2. Add the shrimp and cook, stirring, for 1 minute.

Continued >>

3. Add the fish and cook, stirring, for 1 minute. Then add the snow peas and scallops.

4. Add the noodles and cook (1 minute for fresh, 3 to 4 minutes for dry).

5. Divide the noodles, broth, and seafood among the serving bowls and top each with the kamaboko, scallion, and nori strips.

6. Serve immediately.

Variation: Miso Champon. For a stronger umami flavor, mix ¼ cup Miso Tare (page 41) into the broth before heating it.

ASAHIKAWA RAMEN

Makes 4 bowls   **Prep time: 15 minutes / Cook time: 10 minutes**

Asahikawa, on the island of Hokkaido, is one of the northernmost—and coldest—cities in Japan. As such, this ramen was designed to help locals withstand long arctic winters. In addition to the rich, hearty broths, slices of chashu, and vegetables, this style of ramen has a layer of melted fat floating atop the broth to keep it from cooling off too quickly. Definitely not low-calorie, but very effective at supplying a body with fuel to keep warm.

½ cup Cloudy Chicken Broth (page 36)

4 cups Tonkotsu Pork Broth (page 38)

1 ounce dried shiitake mushrooms, sliced

½ cup Shoyu Tare (page 43)

12 (¼-inch-thick) slices Chashu Pork (page 48)

1 pound fresh or Homemade Ramen Noodles (page 46), **or 8 ounces dried noodles**

4 ounces menma

2 Ajitama Eggs (page 52), halved lengthwise

½ cup sliced scallion, green and white parts

4 tablespoon melted fat (such as lard, beef tallow, or schmaltz), divided

1. In a large saucepan over medium heat, bring the chicken broth, pork broth, and mushrooms to a simmer.

2. Remove the rehydrated mushrooms from the broth and divide among the serving bowls.

3. Add 2 tablespoons of tare to each bowl.

Continued >>

4. In a large dry skillet over medium-high heat, sear the chashu on both sides, about 3 minutes, until light golden brown. Set aside.

5. Bring a large stockpot full of water to a boil over high heat. Add the noodles and boil (1 minute for fresh, 3 to 4 minutes for dry), then drain.

6. Just before the noodles are done, ladle the broth into the bowls. Add the noodles to each bowl and stir gently, mixing the noodles, tare, mushrooms, and broth.

7. Top each bowl with the chashu, menma, half an egg, scallion, and 1 tablespoon of melted fat.

8. Serve immediately.

Variation: Asahikawa Miso. Substitute 1 tablespoon Miso Tare (page 41) for the shoyu tare to give this a different flavor profile.

Cooking tip: If you don't want to pour bacon grease over your ramen, you can substitute salted butter or sesame oil. For some added heat, use spicy sesame oil or chili oil.

TSUKEMEN, PAGE 134

EIGHT

UNCOMMON RAMEN

Although traditional Japanese ramen has four components, steaming broth, flavorful tare, chewy noodles, and toppings, this may not always be the case. Think back to the final ramen rule in chapter 1, "The final rule is: You make the rules." Anything goes! This chapter will introduce you to a number of ramen recipes that change up the traditional ways of preparing and eating ramen. Some of these innovations are in response to changes in the seasons. Other departures from traditional ramen recipes are due to influences from different countries and Japanese chefs who adapted or adopted the methods and ingredients for local palates. Some are simply mistakes that enterprising restaurateurs transformed into culinary innovations. Though not "traditional," the following recipes are all tasty and prove the rule that there are no rules when it comes to ramen!

YAMAGATA COLD RAMEN

Makes 4 bowls   **Prep time: 15 minutes / Cook time: 10 minutes**

Steaming bowls of ramen aren't popular during Yamagata's hot, humid summers. In the 1930s, ramen-ya in Yamagata developed cold ramen or *hiyashi chuka* (chilled Chinese noodles). Some restaurants use ice cubes in the broth to keep everything cool, including the fresh summer toppings, which you can also try if you'd like.

1 pound fresh or Homemade Ramen Noodles (page 46), **or 8 ounces dried noodles**

2 large eggs

1 tablespoon vegetable oil

4 pieces imitation crab legs (surimi), cut into strips

8 ounces sliced deli ham, cut into strips

1 medium carrot, julienned

1 medium cucumber, julienned

1 cup bean sprouts

½ cup sliced scallion, green and white parts

4 tablespoons sesame seeds

4 cups Vegan Broth (page 40), **refrigerated**

½ cup Shoyu Tare (page 43), **refrigerated**

1. In a bowl large enough to accommodate the cooked noodles, prepare an ice water bath.
2. Bring a large stockpot full of water to a boil over high heat. Add the noodles and boil (1 minute for fresh, 3 to 4 minutes for dry), then drain.
3. Submerge the cooked noodles in the ice water to cool them off, then drain well.
4. In a small bowl, whisk the eggs.
5. In a large skillet over medium heat, heat the oil and make a thin omelet with the eggs. Cook until set, about 3 minutes. Remove from the heat and cut into thin strips. Set aside.
6. Place a quarter of the cold noodles in each of the serving bowls.

7. Arrange the strips of egg, the crab legs, ham, carrot, and cucumber in the bowls in a circular pattern like the spokes of a wheel meeting in the center, with one ingredient making up each spoke.

8. Sprinkle the bean sprouts and scallions into the center of the bowl. Garnish with the sesame seeds.

9. In a medium bowl, whisk together the broth and the tare and divide among the bowls.

10. Serve immediately.

Variation: Vegan Yamagata. Make this cold ramen vegetarian by substituting sliced tofu for the ham and crab. Other toppings could include corn, peas, julienned daikon (see the Prep Tip on page 121), or other fresh or pickled vegetables.

TANTANMEN

Makes 4 bowls   **Prep time: 15 minutes / Cook time: 10 minutes**

This hot and spicy noodle soup is adapted from Chinese dan dan mein, or dan dan noodles. Dan dan refers to the long poles on which Chinese merchants used to carry their noodles. When the recipe arrived in Japan in the 1800s, it became tantanmen and lost some of its Sichuan spiciness. Tantanmen noodles are boiled in the broth, which is spicier than typical ramen broths.

4 cups Cloudy Chicken
   Broth (page 36)
½ cup Shoyu Tare (page 43)
1 tablespoon dried red
   chili flakes
1 pound ground pork
¼ cup Mayu (page 54)
2 tablespoons soy sauce
2 tablespoons mirin
1 tablespoon spicy
   sesame oil

1 tablespoon (1-inch piece)
   fresh ginger, unpeeled,
   smashed, and chopped
¼ cup tahini
1 pound fresh or Homemade
   Ramen Noodles
   (page 46), or 8 ounces
   dried noodles
4 baby bok choy, stalks
   trimmed and separated

½ cup sliced scallion, green
   and white parts
2 Ajitama Eggs (page 52),
   halved lengthwise
1 cup bean sprouts
4 tablespoons sesame
   seeds

1.   In a large saucepan over high heat, bring the broth, tare, and chili flakes to a boil.

2.   Meanwhile, in a large skillet over medium-high heat, stir-fry the ground pork, mayu, soy sauce, mirin, oil, ginger, and tahini until the pork is cooked through, about 5 minutes. Set aside.

3. Add the noodles to the boiling broth and cook (1 minute for fresh, 3 to 4 minutes for dry).

4. Place 1 bok choy in the bottom of each serving bowl.

5. Add the noodles and broth to the bowls. Then top with the pork mixture, scallion, half an egg, bean sprouts, and sesame seeds.

6. Serve immediately.

Variation: Spicy Tantanmen. To bring this recipe back to its roots, enhance the heat by adding ¼ cup of rice vinegar to the broth. The vinegar will send the spiciness up into your head, in addition to being in your throat.

TSUKEMEN

Makes 4 bowls   **Prep time: 15 minutes / Cook time: 10 minutes**

Think of this dish as a deconstructed ramen bowl. The components are present but they are not combined into one bowl. The diner decides how to put it all together—or not. *Tsukemen* means "dipping noodles" in Japanese. It was invented in 1961 by Kazuo Yamagishi, a restaurateur in Tokyo, as a way to enjoy ramen even in the summer heat. Robust udon or soba buckwheat noodles are used here. The broth has a more concentrated flavor than the usual ramen broth, as it is intended more for dipping the noodles than for drinking.

3 cups Tonkotsu Pork Broth (page 38)

½ cup Shoyu Tare (page 43)

½ cup Miso Tare (page 41)

1 dozen medium shrimp, peeled, deveined, and halved lengthwise

4 (¼-inch-thick) slices kamaboko (steamed fish cake)

2 Ajitama Eggs (page 52), halved lengthwise

½ cup sliced scallion, green and white parts

1 sheet nori, cut into 3-by-½-inch strips

1 cup bean sprouts

1 pound fresh udon noodles, or 8 ounces dried noodles

1. In a saucepan over high heat, bring the broth, shoyu tare, and miso tare to a simmer.
2. Poach the shrimp in the broth-tare mixture until they curl, about 2 minutes. Once poached, turn off the heat, remove the shrimp from the broth, rinse in ice water, and place in a bowl, along with the kamaboko, eggs, scallion, nori strips, and bean sprouts.
3. In a large bowl, prepare an ice water bath.

4. Bring a large stockpot full of water to a boil over high heat. Add the noodles and boil (1 minute for fresh, 3 to 4 minutes for dry), drain, then cool immediately in the ice bath. Once cooled, drain well, and add the noodles to the bowl with the toppings. Each diner can choose their own toppings for their separate bowls.

5. Distribute the hot broth among the bowls.

6. Serve immediately.

Variations: Wild Card Tsukemen. Any combinations of traditional ramen broths, tare, and toppings can be used in tsukemen. Be creative! Substitute or add any cold or pickled vegetables to your cool topping dish. Thinly sliced cold cuts such as ham, roast beef, or chicken cut into ½-inch strips work well for dipping, too. You can also make it vegan by swapping the tonkotsu for a Vegan Broth (page 40) and flavoring it with Miso Tare (page 41) or Shoyu Tare (page 43) and omitting the eggs.

Serving tip: Lift a few strands of cold noodles and completely submerge them in the hot broth before slurping. Follow that with a bite of a topping. Take a sip of your favorite beverage. Repeat until full!

MAZE SOBA

Makes 4 bowls   Prep time: 15 minutes / Cook time: 10 minutes

Maze soba means "mixed noodles" and is another example of how mistakes can sometimes turn out better than the original plan. This brothless ramen was created when the chef at Menya Hanabi tried to make a Nagoya-style ramen, which uses spicy ground pork. After making the pork, he decided it didn't go well with the broth and was about to throw it all out when a part-time worker suggested putting the ground pork on top of the noodles, and voilà—dry ramen was born!

1 pound ground pork

1 tablespoon dried red chili flakes

¼ cup Mayu (page 54)

1 tablespoon spicy sesame oil

1 tablespoon (1-inch piece) fresh ginger, unpeeled, smashed, and chopped

¼ cup Shoyu Tare (page 43)

1 tablespoon cornstarch

1 pound fresh or Homemade Ramen Noodles (page 46), or 8 ounces dried noodles

2 cups shredded napa cabbage

4 large eggs, at room temperature

½ cup chopped scallion, green and white parts

½ cup bean sprouts

1 sheet nori, cut into 3-by-½-inch strips

1. In a large skillet over high heat, stir-fry the ground pork, chili flakes, mayu, oil, and ginger until the pork is cooked, about 5 minutes. Add the tare and cornstarch and stir until glazed, about 3 minutes.

2. Bring a large stockpot full of water to a boil over high heat. Add the noodles and boil (1 minute for fresh, 3 to 4 minutes for dry), then drain. Divide the noodles among the serving bowls.

3. Top with the cabbage. Stir a raw egg into each bowl along with the spicy stir-fried pork.

4. Top the bowls with the scallion, bean sprouts, and nori strips.

5. Serve immediately.

Variation: Vegetarian Maze Soba. Make this a vegetarian recipe by replacing the ground pork with crumbled, extra-firm tofu.

Cooking tip: If you're not comfortable with raw eggs, you can poach the eggs separately in simmering water or broth by gently floating the eggs in the liquid until the whites are cooked and the yolks are warm but still soft enough to break in the noodles to make a sauce, about 2 minutes.

LEMON RAMEN

Makes 4 bowls   **Prep time: 15 minutes / Cook time: 10 minutes**

This style of ramen is the signature dish at Rinsuzu Shokudo in Tokyo. It's an interesting blend of flavors, with lemons, shoyu tare, and vegan and chicken broths. It's also a simple ramen, as far as toppings go, with only chicken karaage and a sprinkling of scallion.

1 cup **Shoyu Tare** (page 43)

1 cup **Vegan Broth** (page 40)

2 cups **Clear Chicken Broth** (page 34)

1 pound **fresh or Homemade Ramen Noodles**

(page 46), **or 8 ounces dried noodles**

4 small lemons, sliced into ¼-inch circles, ends discarded

12 pieces **Chicken Karaage** (page 50)

½ cup **chopped scallion**

1. In a large saucepan over medium heat, bring the tare, vegan broth, and chicken broth to a simmer.
2. Bring a large stockpot full of water to a boil over high heat. Add the noodles and boil (1 minute for fresh, 3 to 4 minutes for dry), then drain.
3. Divide the broth among the serving bowls and add the noodles to the bowls.
4. Arrange the lemons to float atop the broth and noodles.

5. Top each bowl with the chicken and scallion.

6. Serve immediately.

Variation: Hot and Sour Ramen. Try mixing and matching slices of lime, small oranges, or tangerines. Add some spicy sesame oil for a hot and sour soup.

Cooking tip: To keep the broth from becoming overly sour, remove some (or all) of the lemons as desired.

SEAFOOD TOMATO RAMEN VARIATION, PAGE 142

TOMATO RAMEN

Makes 4 bowls   **Prep time: 15 minutes / Cook time: 10 minutes**

Taiyo No Tomato-men is a chain of ramen-ya that opened in 2006 that specializes in tomato ramen. *Taiyo* means "sun" in Japanese and *men* is "noodles." The broth is a combination of tomatoes and chicken broth. Although the usual toppings of chashu and ajitama are available, the favorite toppings in Japan are grated cheese and basil.

1 (14-ounce) can
   tomato sauce
1 cup Clear Chicken Broth
   (page 34) **or Cloudy
   Chicken Broth** (page 36)

1 cup Tonkotsu Pork Broth
   (page 38)
1 pound fresh or Homemade
   Ramen Noodles
   (page 46), **or 8 ounces
   dried noodles**

16 fresh basil leaves
12 pieces Chicken Karaage
   (page 50)
Grated Parmesan cheese,
   for serving

1. In a large saucepan over high heat, bring the tomato sauce, chicken broth, and tonkotsu broth to a simmer.
2. Bring a large stockpot full of water to a boil over high heat. Add the noodles and boil (1 minute for fresh, 3 to 4 minutes for dry), then drain.
3. Divide the broth among serving the bowls, and place the noodles in each bowl.

Continued >>

4. Top each bowl with 4 basil leaves, chicken, and cheese to taste.

5. Serve immediately.

Variations: Seafood Tomato Ramen. Shrimp, fish, or scallops work well with this. Lightly poach the seafood in the broth for 2 minutes just before dividing it among the bowls.

Vegetarian: Tomato Ramen. Use the Vegan Broth (page 40) with Shoyu Tare (page 43). For the toppings, fry up some eggplant or extra-firm tofu in vegetable oil with a couple of table-spoons of soy sauce, 1 tablespoon of crushed chopped fresh ginger, and 1 garlic clove.

GENMAICHA RAMEN

Makes 4 bowls   **Prep time: 15 minutes / Cook time: 10 minutes**

Matcha is a powdered green tea originating in China and brought to Japan in the 10th century by Buddhist monks. Today, matcha is used as a beverage and as a flavoring. Genmaicha is a combination of matcha and roasted brown rice with a nutty, sweet flavor. Genmaicha works well with a light-flavored vegan broth. It can be found as a mixture of loose tea and toasted rice, in teabags, and as a powder.

2 cups **Vegan Broth** (page 40)

2 cups brewed **genmaicha tea**

1 ounce **tree ear mushrooms, shredded**

4 tablespoons **Miso Tare** (page 41)

4 tablespoons **Mayu** (page 54)

1 pound **silken tofu, cut into 1-inch cubes**

1 pound **fresh or Homemade Ramen Noodles** (page 46)**, or 8 ounces dried noodles**

4 ounces **pickled ginger**

1 cup **bean sprouts**

½ cup **chopped scallion, green and white parts**

4 tablespoons **sesame seeds**

1. In a large saucepan over medium heat, bring the broth, tea, and mushrooms to a simmer.
2. Place 1 tablespoon each of tare and mayu into each serving bowl.
3. Distribute the mushrooms and broth among the bowls. Then, add the tofu.

Continued >>

4. Bring a large stockpot full of water to a boil over high heat. Add the noodles and boil (1 minute for fresh, 3 to 4 minutes for dry), then drain.

5. Divide the noodles among the bowls.

6. Top each bowl with the pickled ginger, bean sprouts, scallion, and sesame seeds.

7. Serve immediately.

Variation: Genmaicha Kare. Substituting Kare (Curry) Coconut Tare (page 44) for the miso tare will give the broth a spicy kick. If you're not concerned about keeping vegan, you could poach shrimp, scallops, or a mild white fish, such as haddock or cod, in the broth for 2 minutes before distributing it among the bowls.

MEASUREMENT CONVERSIONS

WEIGHT EQUIVALENTS

U.S. Standard	Metric (approximate)
½ ounce	15 g
1 ounce	30 g
2 ounces	60 g
4 ounces	115 g
8 ounces	225 g
12 ounces	340 g
16 ounces or 1 pound	455 g

OVEN TEMPERATURES

Fahrenheit	Celsius (approximate)
250°F	120°C
300°F	150°C
325°F	165°C
350°F	180°C
375°F	190°C
400°F	200°C
425°F	220°C
450°F	230°C

VOLUME EQUIVALENTS, LIQUID

U.S. Standard	U.S. Standard (ounces)	Metric (approximate)
2 tablespoons	1 fl. oz.	30 mL
¼ cup	2 fl. oz.	60 mL
½ cup	4 fl. oz.	120 mL
1 cup	8 fl. oz.	240 mL
1½ cups	12 fl. oz.	355 mL
2 cups or 1 pint	16 fl. oz.	475 mL
4 cups or 1 quart	32 fl. oz.	1 L

VOLUME EQUIVALENTS, DRY

U.S. Standard		Metric (approximate)
⅛ teaspoon	—	0.5 mL
¼ teaspoon	—	1 mL
½ teaspoon	—	2 mL
¾ teaspoon	—	4 mL
1 teaspoon	—	5 mL
1 tablespoon	—	15 mL
¼ cup	—	59 mL
⅓ cup	—	79 mL
½ cup	—	118 mL
⅔ cup	—	156 mL
¾ cup	—	177 mL
1 cup	—	235 mL
2 cups or 1 pint	—	475 mL
3 cups	—	700 mL
4 cups or 1 quart	—	1 L
½ gallon	—	2 L

RESOURCES

If you're interested in digging a little deeper to learn more about ramen, a quick search online will bring up hundreds of ramen-related sites. Here are a handful that might be interesting to you.

Websites

Japan-Guide.com Japan Guide is for travelers wanting a rundown of all things Japanese, including ramen.

SeriousEats.com Serious Eats shares tons of ramen recipes and interesting conversations about cooking.

JustOneCookbook.com/japanese-ramen -guide A ramen guide for beginners with very accessible and helpful videos.

Raumen.co.jp/english The Yokohama Ramen Museum has ramen facts, history, and interactive displays.

Ramen Tools and Supplies

FoodAndWine.com/lifestyle/kitchen /ramen-tools This article reviews most of the tools mentioned in this book.

JapanCentre.com/en Here's a store with an extensive inventory. Although it is based in the UK, you can price in dollars.

WebstaurantStore.com This is a site catering to restaurants. Their prices are lower than well-known brick and mortar retailers.

AsianFoodGrocer.com This provider of Asian food is based in California and ships everywhere.

INDEX

ACKNOWLEDGMENTS

Thanks to my patient and tenacious wife, Joan, who regularly inquired whether I was planning on writing today, tomorrow, or sometime soon. When I had procrastinated long enough she asked when the next deadline was. And when it was imminent she stepped in, whisking away anything that beeped, vibrated, or flashed. Without Joan, you would not be reading anything written by me.

A big shout-out to our children, Alex, Cameron, and Lindsay, for their encouragement, support, and amusement as I periodically asked for their advice and to check my memory through them.

Thanks also to my editor, Anna Pulley, at Callisto Media whose positive attitude and great feedback always made my writing better.

Finally, thanks to all you home cooks who picked up my first and second books, *Easy Chinese Cookbook: Restaurant Favorites Made Simple* and *Easy 30-Minute Stir-Fry Cookbook: 100 Asian Recipes for Your Wok or Skillet*. When you shared how much you enjoyed the recipes, posted pictures, or asked questions you made my day!

ABOUT THE AUTHOR

Chris Toy has been teaching Asian cooking for over 30 years. Adopted by Alfred and Grace Toy, a Chinese American couple, he arrived in the United States from Hong Kong in 1958. Toy grew up near Boston, graduating from Quincy Public Schools, Bowdoin College, and Brown University where he earned a master's degree in teaching. A retired teacher, principal, and international educational consultant, he learned Asian cooking in his family's home and restaurant kitchens. As an adult he has explored and become skilled at creating new Asian recipes that incorporate fresh local ingredients. Toy started teaching Asian cooking on weekends at a local kitchen store in Portland, Maine, to make extra money supplementing his first job teaching high school social studies. The combination of teaching and cooking immediately resonated with him. Today, in addition to teaching regularly at local kitchen stores, he teaches adult education classes in several communities around Bath, Maine, where he lives with his wife, Joan. His popular hands-on classes are built around his teaching skills and deep appreciation for fresh, simply prepared food. Toy's cooking incorporates straightforward methods, fresh ingredients, and unique flavors. He especially enjoys drawing family and friends together to share great food and company. A registered Maine guide, Toy enjoys hiking, biking, kayaking, and camping in the woods and waters of Maine's great outdoors. Of course, preparing and sharing good food is always a highlight of his excursions. You can find him at ChrisToy.net or on his YouTube cooking channel: YouTube.com/user/cmtoy.